# Raymond Chandler

## RECOGNITIONS

detective/suspense · science fiction

## Dick Riley, General Editor

*Ray Bradbury*
By Wayne L. Johnson

*Raymond Chandler*
By Jerry Speir

*Critical Encounters: Writers and Themes in Science Fiction*
Dick Riley, Editor

*Frank Herbert*
By Timothy O'Reilly

*Ross Macdonald*
By Jerry Speir

*Dorothy L. Sayers*
By Dawson Gaillard

*Sons of Sam Spade: The Private Eye Novel in the '70s*
By David Geherin

# Raymond Chandler

Jerry Speir

Frederick Ungar Publishing Co. / New York

*To Dick, Marcia, and Ian*

Copyright © 1981 by Frederick Ungar Publishing Co., Inc.
Printed in the United States of America
Designed by Anita Duncan

Library of Congress Cataloging in Publication Data

Speir, Jerry, 1946–
    Raymond Chandler.

    Bibliography: p.
    Includes index.
    1.   Chandler, Raymond, 1888–1959—Criticism and
interpretation.   2.   Detective and mystery stories,
American—History and criticism.
PS3505.H3224Z85          813'.52          80–22589
ISBN 0–8044–2826–3
ISBN 0–8044–6872–9 (pbk.)

# Contents

# Clues to the Reader

While researching this book I happened to overhear one bookstore patron explaining to another that his wife had recently read *The Little Sister* and "like all Chandler's stuff" it was "about homosexuals beating each other to death with coathangers." Whatever the wife may have read, thought, or reported she read, the fact remains that there is no such scene in *The Little Sister*—or anywhere else in Chandler for that matter. But the incident calls attention to the many misconceptions that surround this man's work.

Some people will tell you that Chandler was a misogynist; others will argue that his detective, Marlowe, is homosexual; and still others will insist that Chandler was incapable of constructing a coherent plot. Despite such negative characterizations, his stories continue to enjoy great popularity and have had a profound effect on a major subgenre of American fiction. Discounting the misconceptions and providing some insight into this continuing influence are the two primary intents of this book.

Chandler's uniqueness—and the source of his popularity—is the product of a wide variety of personal traits and talents, circumstances and coincidences. He brought to his work a European sensibility and education supported by a bedrock of childhood experiences in the American Great Plains of the late nineteenth century. He arrived in California while the pioneering spirit still thrived and

witnessed the rise of the movie studios and the attendant exploita-
tion of glamour and illusion. He barely survived the First World
War and was just achieving the peak of his writing career as Western civilization threatened to fall apart in the Second.

Given his far-ranging experience, it is perhaps remarkable that
he maintained the conviction throughout it all that "the best way to
comment on large things is to comment on small things." The "small
things" that preoccupied him were character and language. By concentrating on the motives of individual characters, he approaches
such larger themes as the unpredictability of human emotion under
pressure and the manner in which changing times appear to alter
one's ethical possibilities. He illuminates the way in which characters are alternately responsible for the world in which they live
and trapped by that world. As Dostoevsky reminded us in *Crime
and Punishment,* "this damnable psychology cuts both ways." The
reactions of Chandler's characters to their psychic binds imply the
pervasive instability at the core of modern society. And the language by which these characters reveal themselves allows the author to convey a sense of the delicate web by which we are all
bound together.

The most significant "small things" that occupy Chandler are
the mind and actions of his detective, Philip Marlowe. Marlowe is
a microcosm of both Chandler's concern for character and his concern for the language by which that character is expressed. It is
Marlowe's voice, of course, that is the constant ground of Chandler's stories. It is the detached, ironic, frequently alienated tone
of that voice that holds our attention and provides an interpretive
framework for the tales.

But while we may feel we know Marlowe's voice almost instinctively, a close examination of the novels reveals very little of a "fac-
tual" nature about the detective. We know a few details about his
surroundings, almost nothing about his past, and very little about his
personal motives. We almost never see his mind working, except as
that mental activity is translated into dramatic action. And yet, we
identify with him.

Understanding that identification may be as close as we can
come to appreciating Chandler's power and uniqueness as a writer.
And comprehending what Chandler called his "objective method" is
essential to that appreciation.

The method is further elaborated in the text, but it is most apparent, and perhaps most successful, in Chandler's creation of his detective hero. Finally, we only know Marlowe from the outside. At the end of *The Big Sleep*, for example, we know virtually nothing about Marlowe's state of mind; all we know is that he "stopped at a bar and had a couple of double Scotches" which "didn't do me any good." But from our own experiences of turning, uselessly, to drink in the face of adversity, we sense that we understand this man's predicament and we empathize with him. Chandler's method succeeds because his devotion to objective, physical detail constructs a believable world while his scrupulous avoidance of the subjective allows us, as readers, our own entry into the story, allows us to share imaginatively in Marlowe's dejection that the world is not a better place. And it is that creation of imaginative space that is a mark of Chandler's achievement.

Marlowe's very centrality, then, can be seen as explanation for Chandler's popularity and for his artistic success. But that success also has a double edge. And, as this book goes on to argue, contradictorily, that centrality is also a measure of his failure. Marlowe is finally too stylized a creation to permit growth and development. It is not a problem of which Chandler was unaware.

His concern for language and the writing process itself reflects a similar problem. Here, too, there is the double edge, what might even be called a theme of ambivalence. Throughout all his novels there is a sense of burlesque, as he put it, of parody, of the very form in which he is working and of all its antecedents. The detective form, finally, was of little or no interest to him. And yet, he clearly demonstrates that we are all shaped by our perceptions and uses of forms. Marlowe, for example, frequently finds distraction in chess. His fascination is not unlike our contemporary fascination with football or any number of other games in which we perceive the complexity and unpredictability of life reflected within the manageable confines of rigidly limiting rules. Such games provide a shield of order from the disorder of existence. And, despite our sense of the artificiality of the form, something fundamental drives us to "play the game." The mystery story, for Chandler, offers a similar kind of shield. It promises to order all its disparate elements within the limits of a neatly turned resolution. But in Chandler's hands, it never quite attains such neatness. Chandler the artist is forever rebelling against the restrictions of his chosen genre. Always there is a question at the end. The mystery continues. And Chandler is a mystery writer on the grandest scale.

It is hoped that the following pages will help elucidate the man and his novels. Chapter 1 is a brief biography. Those interested in more details on the subject are directed to Frank MacShane's *The Life of Raymond Chandler,* an excellent book to which any student of Chandler must feel a great debt. Chapters 2 through 4 examine the novels individually in the order of their publication. The reader should be warned that I have found it necessary to discuss the resolutions of *The Big Sleep, Farewell, My Lovely,* and *The Long Goodbye* in considerable detail. Chapter 5 takes a backward glance at Chandler's short stories and examines his development through this early raw material. Marlowe is the subject of Chapter 6, but his influence is so pervasive in Chandler's scheme that he is, in fact, a central subject of most of the book. Chapter 7 takes a closer look at Chandler's style, and the final chapter concentrates on his themes and dark vision. A bibliography, with some annotations, offers a guide to the materials that have been central to my research and that should assist any future student of Chandler. Notes are keyed to phrases and page numbers; no superscript numbers appear in the text.

Numerous people deserve credit for making this book possible. My wife, Barbara Ewell, merits special thanks for her untiring support and critical acumen. My editor, Dick Riley, got me into this muddle and, with his patience, humor, and professional counsel, saw me through it. And a host of friends helped me talk out my ideas. I am particularly indebted to Martin Adamo, Donald McNabb, Edward Murphy, Teresa Toulouse, Harold Weber, and Michael Zimmerman. I only hope that my efforts are worthy of all the kind assistance I have received.

J.S.

*Oxford, Mississippi*
*May 1980*

# 1

# "A Lonely Old Eagle"— Raymond Chandler's Life

"I have lived my life on the edge of nothing."
*Letter, July 25, 1957*

Raymond Thornton Chandler, a figure now assuming legendary proportions as one of the creators of the American "hard-boiled" detective mystery, died a sad and lonely man on the afternoon of March 26, 1959. His subsequent burial in San Diego, California, was attended by only seventeen people. Such isolation in death was a function of the privacy in which he lived out his life. His relative seclusion was perhaps only the natural response of an intense and sensitive man who had endured difficult family relationships, a traumatizing war experience, success and failure as a business executive, and a literary career that confined him to a genre which he alternately loved and longed to escape. And the combined weight of all his alienating experiences must be considered if we are to comprehend his essential dualism of mind, a dualism which perpetually balanced an innate romanticism against a very self-conscious cynicism. In one of his more telling remarks, Chandler commented, "There must be idealism, but there must also be contempt," and it was from his recognition of his own contradictory impulses as emblematic of an age that his fiction took its unique tone.

1

Any effort, therefore, to appreciate the fiction of Raymond Chandler must first seek to understand the peculiar shape of his biography.

Chandler was born in Chicago on July 23, 1888, of an Irish mother and a Pennsylvania Quaker father whose own Irish fore-bears had settled in this country in the seventeenth and eighteenth centuries. His father, Maurice Benjamin Chandler, met his mother, Florence Dart Thornton, in Omaha, Nebraska. She had just come from Ireland to visit her sister Grace in the nearby town of Platts-mouth; Grace had recently married a man named Ernest Fitt. Maurice Chandler was working for a railroad company in Omaha at the time, and traveling the Great Plains and Northwest. On July 25, 1887, Florence and Maurice were married in Laramie, Wyoming, and shortly moved to Chicago where Raymond was born. His father continued to travel with his railroad job while Raymond and his mother summered in Plattsmouth visiting the Fitts, and resided the rest of the year in Chicago.

His father was a notorious drinker (Chandler later referred to him as an "utter swine") and his parents' relationship deteriorated. When Raymond was seven, his mother divorced his father, and she and the young boy sailed for England. Chandler never saw his father again. Mother and son moved into a house in Upper Nor-wood, a suburb south of London, with the mother's sister Ethel and, in Chandler's words, "my stupid and arrogant grandmother."

This is the household, then, within which Chandler grew to maturity. In 1900, the entire household moved to Dulwich so that Raymond could attend the public school there. Natasha Spender, an acquaintance of Chandler in his later years, has spoken of this living arrangement as

> a middle-class household of high Victorian rectitude, where they [Chandler and his mother] were made to feel like disgraced poor relations. . . . From his reminiscences it seemed clear that at far too early an age he was made to feel that he was 'the man in the family' in this household of women, at the same time protecting his mother and sharing the humiliations she suffered from the moralizing condescension of his aunt and grandmother. . . . In the cold moralistic atmosphere of the Dulwich household he could hardly have failed to acquire a self-punishing conscience so that he was not only anxious, but also anxious to succeed, to gain approval.

No doubt these early experiences contributed not only to Chandler's anxieties but also to his fiction where the conflict between two women is often a central structural motif.

At Dulwich, Chandler studied both classical and modern subjects under schoolmasters who were sticklers for clear prose. Moreover, they instilled in their students a strict moral code which embodied both Christian and classical virtues. Dulwich, of course, was in no way atypical of English public schools in this, but it was clearly the initial formative influence on both the sense of literary style and the ethical system which we see reflected in Chandler's novels. He once commented, later in life, "It would seem that a classical education might be rather a poor basis for writing novels in a hard-boiled vernacular. I happen to think otherwise. A classical education saves you from being fooled by pretentiousness, which is what most current fiction is too full of."

Along with the general ethic which Chandler acquired at Dulwich, he also received solid instruction in the craft of writing. One common practice at the school was to have students translate from Latin to English and, then after some interval, to translate the same passage back to Latin. Students were also required to do considerable rewriting of their own compositions. Much later, when Chandler was working at teaching himself the detective format, he used similar methods to perfect this new skill—spending long hours cutting others' stories down to their bare bones and then building them up again in his own style—rewriting and rewriting continually.

When Chandler graduated from Dulwich, he had many ambitions. In addition to writing, he considered going on to one of the universities and becoming a barrister, but there was not enough money for that. Instead, the family decided that he should make a career of the civil service and, further, that he should spend a year abroad, in France and Germany, to prepare for the rigorous civil service examinations. Of this period, Chandler has reported, "I was a bit passive about the whole thing, since I wanted to be a writer and that would not have gone down at all, especially with my rich and tyrannical uncle."

This was only the beginning of the postponement and frustration of his writing ambitions. At the age of seventeen, Chandler found himself alone in Paris, enrolled in a business college and concentrating on learning commercial French. But, as his biographer Frank MacShane has noted, "he was enough of a rebel to imagine himself a comparative philologist, and on his own he dabbled in such recherché languages as modern Greek, Armenian, and Hungarian. Over his bed at the pension he also kept a chart of the 214 key ideographs of Mandarin Chinese." Already his fascination with language was apparent.

Another significant development of this period involved Chandler's English and American acquaintances and his recognition, from this "expatriated" point of view, that he felt totally at home with neither group. He observed that the Americans did seem to enjoy themselves more than their "stuffy" English counterparts. "But," he said, "I wasn't one of them. I didn't even speak their language. I was, in effect, a man without a country." This sense of himself as an outsider plagued Chandler throughout his life. In his personal experience, it contributed to his bouts of bitter loneliness and to his virtually self-imposed social isolation; in his fiction, it is evident in Philip Marlowe's peculiar wit and distant tone.

After Paris, Chandler moved on to Germany where he was apparently more comfortable (partly because his German was better than his French), but he recognized that "there wasn't much sense living in Germany, since it was an open secret, openly discussed, that we would be at war with them almost any time now."

In 1907, then, Chandler returned to London where he was naturalized a British subject in order to be eligible for the civil service. (This action would, much later, cause him considerable financial difficulties between the competing tax authorities of the United States and England.) The exam itself required six days, and when it was over Chandler had placed third overall from among six hundred candidates and first in the classics exam.

His first position was as Assistant Store Officer, Naval Stores Branch, under the Controller of the Navy. It was a clerical and record-keeping job, but, though he retained an aptitude for figures and detail throughout his life, Chandler resigned after six months. He still wanted to write; his family was outraged.

Nevertheless, he did finally begin to explore his writing ambitions. His first job after the Admiralty was that of reporter for the *Daily Express* where "I was a complete flop, the worst man they ever had." But despite this failure, he was able to move on to the *Westminster Gazette,* a leading liberal paper, where he published twenty-seven poems between 1908 and 1912. These early works are of little literary merit except as they foreshadow the author's later development. They are, in MacShane's words, "full of sadly noble subjects and sentiments like death, fairyland, melancholy, art, and meditation." A few titles are sufficient to suggest the tenor of these pieces: "The Unknown Love," "The Perfect Knight," "A Lament for Youth," "Time Shall Not Die." But, slowly, he turned from poetry to prose. At first, his attempts were limited to odd paragraphs translated from French and German papers for inclusion in the *Gazette* and to "sketches, most of a satirical nature— the kind of thing Saki did so infinitely better."

By 1911–12, however, Chandler was contributing articles and reviews to the *Academy,* a literary weekly. In these early essays, we can witness him working out the ideas which age and broader experience would eventually mold into his mature fiction. In the controversy between realism and idealism, for example, he argued that the idealists were of greater merit because "they exalt the sordid to a vision of magic; and create pure beauty out of plaster and vile dust." Reviewing these essays in later years, Chandler commented, quite accurately, that "they are of an intolerable preciousness of style, but already quite nasty in tone."

The year 1912 was a critical one for Chandler. He was twenty-three. Other men his age had had greater success. A friend whom he considered a superior literary talent committed suicide. Chandler himself was evidently deeply affected by a frustrated love interest. Thus, depressed and feeling himself a failure, he borrowed five hundred pounds from his uncle and set sail for his other home, America.

A chance meeting on this fateful voyage to New York profoundly affected the subsequent course of his life. Aboard ship with him were Warren and Alma Lloyd of Los Angeles. Warren held a Ph.D. in philosophy from Yale; Alma was a sculptor. They also happened to be involved in a family oil business in the Los Angeles area and invited Chandler to visit them if he made it to the West Coast. Lacking any real destination, Chandler, not surprisingly, soon accepted the invitation. But first he passed through New York and St.

Louis, and spent some time in Nebraska visiting his Uncle Ernest
and Aunt Grace Fitt.

But then it was on to California,

> with a beautiful wardrobe, a public school accent, no practical
> gifts for earning a living, and a contempt for the natives which,
> I am sorry to say, has in some measure persisted to this day. I
> had a pretty hard time trying to make a living. Once I worked
> on an apricot ranch ten hours a day, twenty cents an hour.
> Another time I worked for a sporting goods house, stringing
> tennis racquets for $12.50 a week, 54 hours a week.

With Warren Lloyd's help, he acquired a job as bookkeeper for the
Los Angeles Creamery. During this period, he was visiting the
Lloyds regularly. Friday evenings at their house were social occasions for literary and philosophical discussion as well as musical entertainment. Alma Lloyd was an accomplished singer and Julian
Pascal, a family friend and frequent guest, was a distinguished
pianist and composer. It was at such gatherings that Chandler first
met Julian's wife Cissy, who was later to become his own wife under
rather trying circumstances.

But at this point, world events intervened in Chandler's life.
The American declaration of war in 1917 finally drew him into that
struggle. In August 1917, Chandler enlisted in the Canadian Army at
Victoria, British Columbia. His choice of the Canadian rather than
the American army was prompted by two considerations. One, as
he later put it, was that "it was still natural for me to prefer a
British uniform." His dual nationality permitted him such a choice.
But secondly, the Canadian Army provided an additional allowance
for his dependent mother who had come to live with him in 1916.
This extra money was no doubt a matter of some importance.

By March 1918, Chandler was on the front lines in France.
Curiously, he wrote very little of these experiences. One brief sketch
called "Trench Raid" survives. It is a third-person narrative of a
man experiencing an artillery barrage in the trenches, and in it we
can glimpse the stark alienation which later informed his detective
fiction: "He seemed to be alone in a universe of brutal noise. The
sky, in which the calendar called for a full moon, was white and
blind with innumerable Very lights, white and blind and diseased

like a world gone leprous." The sketch was based on a real event of June 1918. In that month, Chandler was his unit's sole survivor of a German artillery attack on their position. He never wrote directly on the subject again and was only able to approach such trauma fictionally—and then obliquely—in the character of Terry Lennox in *The Long Goodbye,* one of his last novels. And he only alluded to the war in conversation with friends in rare remarks like, "Once you have had to lead a platoon into direct machine-gun fire, nothing is ever the same again."

But, evidently, neither the artillery barrage nor the awesome responsibility of leading men to their deaths deterred his desire to make his contribution to the war effort. While recuperating in England, he requested transfer to the Royal Air Force for pilot training. But his flying ambitions fell victim to the Armistice, and, on February 20, 1919, he was discharged at Vancouver.

Chandler was then a man of thirty with no clear future before him and no very clear concept of "home." Both Los Angeles and London were possibilities, but nothing compelled him to either. For a while, he simply drifted about the American Northwest, and, as he put it, "had another feeble fling at writing and almost sold the *Atlantic* a Henry James pastiche, but . . . didn't get anywhere." He eventually took a job in the San Francisco branch of a London bank, perhaps hoping to get transferred to the home office. But the job didn't last. He was then a reporter for six weeks for the Los Angeles *Daily Express.* And throughout this period he was moving regularly, establishing what MacShane calls a pattern of "habitual rootlessness" that persisted throughout most of his life.

Chandler's return to Los Angeles, of course, meant the renewal of friendships with the Lloyds and the Pascals. Would-be matchmakers had romantic plans for this young, eligible, attractive, veteran bachelor, but none of them were to be fulfilled. Instead, Chandler fell in love with Cissy Pascal, Julian's wife. She was forty-eight at the time, eighteen years Chandler's senior. But Cissy was a strikingly beautiful woman and the gap of years between them was not apparent.

Inevitably, pseudo-psychological commentaries on Chandler make much of this age discrepancy. The impulse is to say something like "Chandler married his mother" and then to use that idea to try to explain the mind and art of the novelist. His biographer,

Frank MacShane, sees little merit in such theories. Rather, he opines that Cissy was a lively, original, intelligent, mature, youthful-looking woman who seemed precisely right for a man of Chandler's age and experience who had tired of wandering. Although they lived together, at least at times, after Cissy's divorce was final in 1920, the couple did not marry until 1924, the year Chandler's mother died. She had strongly objected to the match, and they postponed matrimony in deference to her wishes.

Chandler's business career was also taking a new turn about this time. Through the Lloyds, Chandler had become an employee of the Dabney Oil Syndicate of which Warren Lloyd's brother was a partner. The oil business in Los Angeles was booming. One-fifth of the world's crude, in that era, came from its immediate vicinity.

In 1923, Dabney Oil's auditor was convicted of embezzling, and Chandler got both a new position as assistant auditor and direct experience with the scandalous possibilities of big business. Not long after, he inherited the top position when the new chief auditor died of a heart attack in the office. Perhaps more relevant to his future writing, Chandler had to assist the police in placing the body in the morgue and saw it through the autopsy. It was one of his rare first-hand experiences with the routine procedures of policemen and coroners. Later, when writing his fiction, Chandler relied almost exclusively on books to guide him in matters of technical accuracy. Among them were such titles as Major J. S. Hatcher's *Textbook of Firearms,* a pamphlet called *1,000 Police Questions Answered for the California Peace Officer,* and similar texts on medicine and toxicology. At least once, however, at Dabney Oil, Chandler encountered the real thing.

Shortly after his rise to auditor, he was promoted to vice-president handling contracts, mergers, and purchases of subsidiaries. His salary rose to $1,000 a month and his advancement continued. As he later recalled, "I was an executive in the oil business once, a director of eight companies and a president of three, although actually I was simply a high-priced employee. They were small companies, but very rich. I had the best office staff in Los Angeles and I paid them higher salaries than they could have got anywhere else, and they knew it."

As the tone of that remark suggests, the business world brought out Chandler's tougher, more competitive side. He saw business disputes in terms of legal battles and took pleasure in employing the best lawyers he could find and in knowing the precise strengths of each. MacShane has called attention to "a certain literalness in his solutions to problems that suggests a lonely man who did little consulting before he acted and who was always on guard." His actions began to earn him enemies.

At home, his relationship with Cissy was going through one of its worst periods. As she approached sixty, the age discrepancy became more obvious and her illnesses more frequent. More and more, Chandler was seen at public functions alone.

The pressures of the oil business increased with the onset of the Depression. Combined with his domestic difficulties, the pressures became too great. Chandler began to drink heavily (a reaction to adversity which would recur throughout his life), and he made at least one half-serious attempt at suicide. He also began to have affairs with secretaries in the office, sometimes not returning from a weekend until Wednesday. Finally, his absences extended into weeks when no one could find him.

In 1932, at the age of forty-four, Raymond Chandler was fired. He had been in America twenty years, had experienced considerable success, but now found himself in a situation very like the one in which he arrived. He had nowhere to go, nothing to do. Years later, he would remark about the experience that it "taught me not to take anything for granted." But for a man of his age, with little financial reserve, the experience must have been devastating.

The next year or so found Chandler casting about for a new beginning. He still harbored literary ambitions and began to write poems and short fictional sketches again. Hemingway became a model, as a title of a brief parody from this period, "Beer in the Sergeant Major's Hat, or the The Sun Also Sneezes," suggests. Other American writers with whom he felt a certain kinship were Theodore Dreiser, Ring Lardner, Carl Sandburg, Sherwood Anderson, and Walt Whitman. And on the international scene, he was particularly fond of the works of Flaubert, James, Conrad, Dumas, and Dickens.

For a time, he considered writing for the slick magazines, but he was finally contemptuous of "their fundamental dishonesty in the matter of character and motivation." Turning elsewhere, he began to pick up the popular pulp magazines "because they were cheap enough to throw away" and, as he said, "it suddenly struck me that I might be able to write this stuff and get paid while I was learning."

*Black Mask* was considered the best of these mass market publications since it consistently published the likes of Erle Stanley Gardner and Dashiell Hammett, of whom the latter was a major influence on Chandler's detective fiction. The editor of *Black Mask*, Joseph T. "Cap" Shaw, was largely responsible for developing the policy of the magazine which meshed precisely with Chandler's ideas of craft. In Shaw's formulation, "We wanted simplicity for the sake of clarity, plausibility and belief. We wanted action, but we held that action is meaningless unless it involves recognizable human character in three-dimensional form." He thought his magazine's stories should emphasize "character and the problems inherent in human behavior over crime solution."

The guidelines fit Chandler perfectly. Throughout his career, he spoke of himself as "a poor plotter" and professed an aversion to the detective form's demand for tightly controlled puzzles. On one occasion he remarked that "I have good ideas for about four books, but the labour of shaping them into plots appalls me." On another, he commented that "the mystery and the solution of the mystery are only what I call 'the olive in the martini,' and the really good mystery is one you would read even if you knew somebody had torn out the last chapter." Such comments call attention to Chandler's conception of himself as a stylist, and his first exploration of style within the detective format was published in *Black Mask* in December 1933. It was an 18,000-word story called "Blackmailers Don't Shoot" and caused the editorial staff to wonder if this unknown man were a genius or crazy. The story was so well polished that not a phrase could be cut, thus the praise for his "genius." But in his compulsive drive for perfection, he had also tried to "justify" the right margin, as printers say. He had tried to make the typed page appear with even margins on both the left and right, like a printed page—thus the concern for his possible "craziness." Chandler had worked on the story for five months and was paid the standard rate of a penny a word, $180.

His stories continued to be accepted with little or no alteration, and by 1938 he had published 16 stories and was working on his first novel. Financially, times were bleak, as they were for many people in the Depression. In 1938, Chandler earned only $1,275; he and Cissy had stored their furniture and were living in smaller, furnished rooms to save money.

That first novel, of course, was *The Big Sleep* and, remarkably, it was finished in three months, the shortest time span in which any of the novels were completed. The novel is derived largely from previously published short stories, primarily "Killer in the Rain" and "The Curtain." Chandler referred to this process of incorporating the stories into the novels as "cannibalizing" and used the method to write *Farewell, My Lovely* and *The Lady in the Lake* as well, though it never again worked with such ease and speed.

In March of 1939, Chandler committed a statement to paper which, in no uncertain terms, reveals his conception of his detective mysteries strictly as pot-boilers to allow him to move on to greater things. His note begins: "Since all plans are foolish . . . let us make a plan." It is an outline of work for the next two to three years and beyond. First on the list are plans for four more detective novels. But then come plans for what he calls a "dramatic novel" tentatively titled *English Summer*. It was to be "a short, swift, tense, gorgeously written story verging on melodrama. . . . The surface theme is the American in England, the dramatic theme is the decay of the refined character and its contrast with the ingenuous honest utterly fearless and generous American of the best type." Then the plan proceeds to what he calls "short-long stories" or "fantastic stories," a type about which he often spoke but which he only attempted in "The Bronze Door" and "Professor Bingo's Snuff"— stories in which a person's ability to disappear plays a central role. Cautioning himself that the detective stories must make enough for him to get "two years' money ahead" before stepping outside the genre, he goes on exultantly, "If *English Summer* is a smash hit, which it should be, properly written, written up to the hilt but not overwritten, I'm set for life. From then on I'll alternate the fantastic and the dramatic until I think of a new type. Or may do a suave detective just for the fun." Ultimately, his plan did prove to be somewhat "foolish"—at least it was never realized—but it offers an important insight into Chandler's intentions and self-perceptions, at least in 1939.

Despite the hopeful tone of his plan, however, it was not a good year for Chandler. In May, still seeking to establish his finan-

cial security, he and Cissy moved, impulsively, again—this time to a
cabin at Big Bear Lake where, at an elevation of 7,000 feet, they
could get away from the city and the heat. The mountain lake setting appears, of course, in *The Lady in the Lake*, which he was
writing at the time. He was also working on *Farewell, My Lovely*
simultaneously, and the two works occupied him through the rest
of the year and into 1940. But the writing progressed by fits and
starts, distracted largely by his preoccupation with the war in Eu-
rope. In fact, Chandler volunteered for officer training in the Canadian Army about this time but was rejected because of his age.

The next few years continued to be trying ones: the war
dragged on, Cissy became more prone to illness, and money was a
constant problem. But there were some hopeful signs. In 1941, RKO
bought the film rights to *Farewell, My Lovely*—but the contract (for
$2,000) was one which Chandler later characterized as "of almost
unparalleled stupidity."

His naiveté in dealing with the movie industry was still evident
in 1943 when he was called by Paramount to work with Billy
Wilder on a screenplay of James M. Cain's *Double Indemnity*.
Chandler's response to the offer was that he wanted $1000 and
couldn't possibly have anything ready before the following Mon-
day. The studio was astonished; what they had in mind was a standard thirteen-week contract at $750 a week. Despite Chandler's
total lack of understanding of the realities of the movie industry,
and despite some personal foibles which made him difficult to work
with (Billy Wilder described him as "bad tempered—kind of
acid, sour, grouchy"), the movie was a success and established
Chandler's reputation as a screenwriter. The script, in fact, was
nominated for an Oscar, and Chandler's career was on the upswing.

*The Lady in the Lake* appeared in 1944 and by 1945 Chandler
was back at Paramount with a three-year contract calling for
twenty-six weeks work a year at $1,000 per week with raises. If
taxes are a measure of success, it may be worth noting that Chandler paid $50,000 in income taxes in 1945. But 1945 was also the
year of *The Blue Dahlia*, and that story deserves repeating for the
light it may shed on the elusive character of this enigmatic man.

John Houseman's published recollection of the event begins:
"Raymond Chandler was fifty-seven when he risked his life for me."
Houseman was a director at Paramount, and he and Chandler had

become friends during Chandler's work on *Double Indemnity*, largely on the strength of their being the only graduates of English public schools of all the people on the lot.

In early 1945, Paramount was faced with a problem; Alan Ladd, one of its prime box office attractions, was being called into the military within three months, and the company needed desperately to turn out another vehicle featuring him before his departure. (Normal production schedules at the time required eighteen months from writing through shooting.) Chandler, as was not unusual for him, had several pieces at hand on which he had been working and offered to attempt a hurried adaptation for the screen. His offer was quickly accepted and Chandler delivered the first half of *The Blue Dahlia* within three weeks. But then a difficulty arose. As Houseman, who had been assigned to direct the picture, has put it: "Ray's problem with the script (as with the book) was a simple one: he had no ending."

Shooting had already begun, and the camera was rapidly catching up to the available script. Paramount executives became nervous. One invited Chandler into his office and explained that the project was of such great importance to the studio that he was prepared to offer an additional $5,000 bonus if the script were finished on time. Rather than motivating Chandler, the offer insulted him, undermined his self-confidence, and left him unable to write a word. Alan Ladd was ten days away from his induction into the Army. However, the day after Chandler's announcement that he was no longer capable of finishing the script, his loyalty to his friend Houseman got the better of him, and he offered an "astonishing proposal." He felt that his only chance for finishing the job was to do it at home—and drunk. Chandler had managed, with rare exceptions, to stop drinking and had been off the bottle for over ten years. Previous drinking bouts had endangered his health, but he felt that it was his only chance to meet the deadline. With the aid of round-the-clock secretaries, a physician's supervision, limousines on standby to run copy to the studio, and an open line to the Paramount switchboard, the project was completed. Like *Double Indemnity*, *The Blue Dahlia* received an Oscar nomination.

Two other film contracts in the late 1940s also marked milestones in Chandler's writing career even while intensifying his distaste for the movie industry. In the spring of 1947, Chandler signed a contract with Universal that was a writer's dream. It called for an original screenplay and paid $4,000 a week plus a guaranteed share of the profits. He was given almost unlimited freedom in developing the script and used that freedom to forsake both Los Angeles as setting and Marlowe as hero. Wanting a border town for the locale, he chose Vancouver and replaced Marlowe with a Canadian police officer named Killaine. The screenplay was tentatively called *Playback*. Health problems—both his and Cissy's—interfered with the writing, as did Chandler's general dislike of screenwriting. He was never very pleased with the finished product and neither was the studio. Citing financial difficulties and the expense of filming in Vancouver, the studio shelved the project and forgot it. *Playback* did finally see the light of day in 1958 as Chandler's last, and generally least-regarded, novel. It was rewritten, of course, with California as background and Marlowe as detective hero.

In 1950, Chandler entered into his final attempt at screenwriting in a contract to adapt Patricia Highsmith's *Strangers on a Train* for a Warner Brothers film to be directed by Alfred Hitchcock. Chandler liked the book and thought he would enjoy working with Hitchcock, but their relationship was stormy, and the script finally had to be rewritten by another writer, Czenzi Ormonde. Chandler, reluctantly, retained shared credit for the film.

His confrontations with Hitchcock centered on questions of plausibility and gave him cause to reflect on the differences between writing novels and writing screenplays:

> When you read a story, you accept its implausibilities and extravagances because they are no more fantastic than the conventions of the medium itself. But when you look at real people, moving against a real background, and hear them speaking real words, your imagination is anaesthetised. You accept what you see and hear, but you do not complement it from the resources of your imagination. . . . The modern film tries too hard to be real. Its techniques are so perfect that it requires no contribution from the audience but a mouthful of popcorn.

Hitchcock, for his part, remembered the confrontations in these terms: "We'd sit together and I would say, 'Why not do it this way?' and he'd answer, 'Well, if you can puzzle it out, what do you need me for?'" No doubt a clash of strong-willed personalities was largely responsible for the conflict.

Regardless, one positive consequence of the experience was to leave Chandler feeling at last emancipated enough to proclaim:

> From now on I am going to write what I want to write as I want to write it. Some of it may flop. There are always going to be people who will say I have lost the pace I had once, that I take too long to say things now, and don't care enough about tight active plots. But I'm not writing for those people now. I'm writing for the people who understand about writing as an art and are more able to separate what a man does with words and ideas from what he thinks about Truman or the United Nations (I have a low opinion of both). . . . You have to get some fun out of this job and you can't get it by filling orders.

As well as anticipating his critics, the remark also looks toward the freer construction of *The Long Goodbye* (1953) and underscores the real pressures Chandler had experienced throughout his writing career to stick rather rigidly to a locale, a hero, and a format.

In 1952, Chandler and Cissy took action to escape some of the other pressures of Hollywood and to fulfill an ambition which he had been harboring for over thirty years: they embarked for England. Not surprisingly, given both their ages and their general social awkwardness, the trip was less than a total success. On one occasion Chandler refused to attend a party given in his honor by his London publisher, Hamish Hamilton, because it was suggested that he might wear a dinner jacket, and he hadn't brought one. No amount of persuasion could change his mind—despite the fact that the trip provided Chandler his first meeting with Hamilton after ten years' written correspondence; Chandler was an inveterate letter writer. Though he met numerous celebrities from literary, publishing, and media circles, Chandler seems to have most enjoyed throwing darts in a local pub with some of the men from his publisher's warehouse.

The trip home proved an uncomfortable one and Cissy's health, as well as Chandler's own, deteriorated. In his later years, Chandler suffered from bronchitis, chronic sore throats, and a variety of debilitating skin allergies. One of the latter affected his hands and required him to wear gloves when typing, reading, or handling paper.

Despite these problems, he was able to continue with his writing through much of 1953 and finished *The Long Goodbye* in July of that year. But the following year was devoted largely to caring for Cissy; on December 12, 1954, she died at the age of eighty-four.

Chandler was to live five more unhappy years. Within two months of Cissy's death, he attempted suicide with a pistol and was subsequently hospitalized. Before his death he would be hospitalized several more times for either suicidal depressions or maladies related to alcohol. Drink had again become a serious problem.

Chandler's last years make a sad, pathetic tale. In April of 1955, he set out again for London. Initially, his experience there was a lonely one, but that was finally altered by his meeting Natasha Spender, pianist wife of the poet Stephen Spender. She has noted that when she first met Chandler he was "Sixty-seven years old, still suicidal, very alcoholic and absorbed in what he always called the 'long nightmare' of mourning." With a group of women friends, Spender organized a "shuttle service" to look after him, believing that "his gentlemanly good manners would not permit him to implement his evidently strong suicidal impulses if he had an imminent social engagement with a lady." Spender has also reported that in these last years "his fantasy seemed entirely to be used in acting out romantic Don Quixote illusions." He liked very much to lavish his new lady friends with presents and would invent imaginary dangers from which to protect them. Perhaps the most poignant and telling of episodes from this period concerns an evening when Spender had played a concert with the Bournemouth Symphony Orchestra. After the performance, she was dining with the mayor and town council when Chandler "suddenly arrived white-faced and ghostly in full evening dress with white silk scarf" announcing that he had come to take her home. He had hired a Rolls and laden the back with silver ice buckets, champagne, and carnations to fetch her in royal, fantastic style.

Throughout his novels, Chandler consistently mocks such sentimentality. But even while he mocks it, he suggests that sentimentality is part of the inescapable structure of the human experience. As he and Spender rode back toward London amid such fanciful trappings, Chandler turned to her and said, "I know what you all are doing for me, and I thank you, but the truth is I really *want* to die." It seems evident that he was still capable of appreciating the ironies of an absurd world but that he had simply lost the will to continue. It seems equally evident that, whatever conflicts and difficulties he and Cissy may have shared, she was for him the force that made life worth the effort.

In his last years, he sought hopefully but sadly for someone to replace her loss. But his longing only made him more susceptible to the attractions of at least two much younger women. Marriage was proposed, the proposals retracted, the beneficiary of his will was changed several times, and, ultimately, he looked simply the foolish, gullible, senile old man.

Some stability was salvaged from this disorder by Chandler's London agent, Helga Greene, who flew to meet him in La Jolla in February of 1959. She accompanied him to New York where he accepted the presidency of the Mystery Writers of America, an honor to which he had recently been elected. And she hoped to get him back to London and away from the woman who had been causing such havoc in his life most recently. But it was not to be; another plea from that woman drew him back to California, and it was there he died on March 26, 1959, at the age of seventy.

Chandler's pathetic last years, of course, are not our primary interest. But they do serve as an indicator of the depths of the frustration of this man who was never satisfied to be known simply as a writer of mysteries. He once, in fact, refused an offer of $5,000 for rights to distribute *The Little Sister* to the membership of the Doubleday Mystery Guild; he simply found the category claustrophobic. As late as 1957, he was contemplating such new creative avenues as a play for the English stage, but he did not live to fulfill those dreams. Rather, he is remembered by us as a premiere detective novelist, and the force of those novels owes something, no doubt, to his persistent struggle to get beyond the severe limitations of its form.

He was a man not unlike a description he himself once wrote of Somerset Maugham: "a pretty sad man, pretty lonely. . . . I don't mean that he has no friends. . . . But I don't think they build much of a fire against the darkness for him. He's a lonely old eagle."

# 2

## The First Novels:

### The Big Sleep
### Farewell, My Lovely
### The High Window

"I'm not joking, and if I seem to talk in circles, it just
seems that way. It all ties together—everything."
*The Big Sleep*

Philip Marlowe crackles to life on a cloudy October morning in the
first paragraph of *The Big Sleep* (1939). "I was wearing my
powder-blue suit, with dark blue shirt, tie and display handker-
chief, black brogues, black wool socks with dark blue clocks on
them. I was neat, clean, shaved and sober, and I didn't care who
knew it. I was everything the well-dressed private detective ought
to be. I was calling on four million dollars." Already he exhibits
the wry self-mockery which occupies us throughout the novels. The
tone is self-assured, even cocky, but it also maintains the ironic de-
tachment of a man conscious of his own pose. By the end of the
novel, however, these high spirits will have changed dramatically.
And it is precisely in such alterations of Marlowe's mood and in the
revelations which precipitate them that Chandler imbeds the meaning of his stories. To appreciate this transformation in *The Big
Sleep*, we must first understand the events which prompt it—the
plot, that element about which Chandler claimed to have little
concern.

The plot of this novel has drawn considerable, undeserved

criticism. One critic, Stephen Pendo, has gone so far as to assert that it is "a confused tangle that demonstrates Chandler's problem of producing a cohesive story line," expressing a fairly common judgment. Part of the problem here may derive from what one is willing to accept as cohesive. And part of the problem, particularly as relates to the public's general misconceptions about this story, no doubt relates to interpretations of the popular 1946 film version of the novel rather than to the book itself. While the film is quite successful within its own limits—and Chandler was very pleased with Bogart's portrayal of Marlowe—it achieves much of its mystery and suspense by omitting many of the subplots and explanations of motivation which are critical concerns for Chandler and which he so carefully details in the novel. A general caution is perhaps in order here concerning the use of any of the movies based on Chandler's works as guides for interpreting the novels or the novelist. Most, in fact, stray further from their sources than does the Bogart-Bacall version of *The Big Sleep*.

But, to return to the question of cohesiveness, as relates to Chandler's plots, we should bear in mind his remark that he was always "more intrigued by a situation where the mystery is solved more by the exposition and understanding of a single character . . . than by the slow and sometimes long-winded concatenation of circumstances." It is to character, then, and to the motivations of character that we must look in Chandler if we are to untangle the confusion. And, since the confusion among readers and critics is so widespread, a fairly detailed analysis of the plot seems in order.

The characters who occupy center stage in *The Big Sleep* fall into two echelons: the members and associates of the wealthy Sternwood family and a loosely associated group of racketeers with whom the Sternwoods have inevitably become involved.

The Sternwood family consists of an aging, dying patriarch known as "the General," and his two daughters, Carmen and Vivian, "still in the dangerous twenties." Wrapped in a rug and bathrobe, sitting in a wheelchair amidst the orchids of his sweltering greenhouse, the General describes himself to Marlowe as "a very dull survival of a rather gaudy life" who seems "to exist largely on heat, like a newborn spider." His complaint is that he is "being blackmailed again." As he explains, he has recently "paid a man named Joe

Brody five thousand dollars to let my younger daughter Carmen alone;" he then proceeds to show Marlowe a new demand for $1,000 from a man named Geiger for what Geiger says are gambling debts. Geiger's stationery indicates that he is a dealer in "Rare Books and DeLuxe Editions."

In the course of their conversation, Marlowe gets the General's opinion of his children: "Vivian is spoiled, exacting, smart and quite ruthless. Carmen is a child who likes to pull wings off flies." Marlowe also learns about another member of the family, Rusty Regan, Vivian's third and most recent husband who has disappeared under mysterious circumstances. Regan's past accomplishments include work as a bootlegger and service as an officer in the I.R.A. The General has in fact been quite taken by the young man's tales of the Irish revolution, and Marlowe is soon amused and perplexed to learn that virtually everyone, daughters and police included, assume he has been hired to find Regan.

But, sticking to his primary suspect, Marlowe soon learns that Geiger's real business is a rather high-class lending library of dirty books. He locates Geiger's house and parks outside in the dying light to perform a little surveillance. The rain which has been threatening all afternoon drips through the leaking top of his convertible, and, typically, he turns to a pocket flask in his glove compartment for comfort. Carmen arrives and enters. Shortly afterward a flash of "hard white light" comes from the house in conjunction with a scream—a scream that "had a sound of half-pleasurable shock, an accent of drunkenness, an overtone of pure idiocy. It was a nasty sound." By the time Marlowe gets to the house, three shots have been fired and there is the sound of someone fleeing.

Marlowe's discovery of what has happened is revealed in a manner that is virtually a trademark of Chandlerian exposition. After building suspense with mysterious flashes, sudden gunfire, and an unidentified person running away, Chandler opens our first look at the scene with one of Marlowe's characteristically deadpan remarks: "Neither of the two people in the room paid any attention to the way I came in, although only one of them was dead." As we begin to read that statement, we sense that at least some of the suspense is about to be resolved. But its last phrase brings us up abruptly with the recognition that our expectations were too simplistic. Thus chastened, and with a smile for the author's almost perverse sense of comic relief, we attend more warily to Marlowe's typically dispassionate survey of the room and its every detail:

> It had a low beamed ceiling . . . brown plaster walls decked out with strips of Chinese embroidery and Chinese and Japanese prints . . . a thick pinkish Chinese rug . . . bits of old silk tossed around, as if whoever lived there had to have a piece he could reach out and thumb . . . a black desk with carved gargoyles at the corners and behind it a yellow satin cushion on a polished black chair with carved arms and back . . . the pungent aftermath of cordite and the sickish aroma of ether.

Only after that exhaustive catalogue do we get any information about what most interests us, the people.

> On a sort of low dais at one end of the room there was a high-backed teakwood chair in which Miss Carmen Sternwood was sitting on a fringed orange shawl. She was sitting very straight, with her hands on the arms of the chair, her knees close together, her body stiffly erect in the pose of an Egyptian goddess, her chin level, her small bright teeth shining between her parted lips. Her eyes were wide open. The dark slate color of the iris had devoured the pupil. They were mad eyes. She seemed to be unconscious, but she didn't have the pose of unconsciousness. She looked as if, in her mind, she was doing something very important and making a fine job of it. Out of her mouth came a tinny chuckling noise which didn't change her expression or even move her lips.
>     She was wearing a pair of long jade earrings. They were nice earrings and had probably cost a couple of hundred dollars. She wasn't wearing anything else.

Geiger, we are told after a similarly lengthy description, "was very dead."

This very calculated pacing serves several functions. First of all, it impresses us with the detective's method: having access only to objective data, he must weigh all details equally if he is to avoid overlooking one that might prove critical. But, more importantly, for Marlowe himself such pacing and apparent concern for objectivity provide a necessary check on his own subjective sensibilities. This kind of emotional control is further related to Chandler's notion of an "objective method" of writing in which dialogue and description become vehicles of emotion (see Chapter 7). That is, Chandler—and Marlowe—recognize that subjectivity is the ground of human experience and motivation, rather than objective reality. But, any one individual—Marlowe or the reader—has only the external indications of that subjectivity, that inner activity, from which to draw conclusions about any particular person. It was Chandler's desire to convey emotion and character not by *describing* them, but by *demonstrating* them through dialogue and physical details. A continued analysis of the plot and of Chandler's manner of relating it should enlighten the point.

Following Geiger's death, Marlowe discovers that the books from his store are being moved to the apartment of Joe Brody, the man whom the General mentioned as a recipient of $5,000 of his blackmail money. Agnes, the woman who worked in Geiger's store, is evidently assisting Brody in his plot to take over the business.

Back at Geiger's house, Marlowe runs into Eddie Mars, whom he describes with the same detached thoroughness as he had the furniture. He is

> a gray man, all gray, except for his polished black shoes and two scarlet diamonds in his gray satin tie that looked like the diamonds on roulette layouts. His shirt was gray and his double-breasted suit of soft, beautifully cut flannel. Seeing Carmen he took a gray hat off and his hair underneath it was gray and as fine as if it had been sifted through gauze. His thick gray eyebrows had that indefinably sporty look. He had a long chin, a nose with a hook to it, thoughtful gray eyes that had a slanted look because the fold of skin over his upper lid came down over the corner of the lid itself.

His "colorlessness" is also a characteristic of Chandler's descriptive technique and, as we will see later (Chapter 7), another device by which he imparts meaning.

Mars is the operator of The Cypress Club, a local gambling establishment, and considers himself just a businessman. He claims to own the house in which Geiger was living and says he was just passing by to check on his tenant. But Marlowe is skeptical. He has already learned that Mars is also a good friend of Vivian Sternwood and that he has, in fact, financed some of her gambling sprees. It also appears that there was more connection between Mars and Geiger than the simple tenant–landlord relationship. If nothing else, Geiger's was a business that needed protection and Mars was the man with the contacts and power to deliver it. But the exact nature of their relationship must await further development.

Marlowe shortly finds his attention occupied by a small man with "tight brilliant eyes that wanted to look hard, and looked as hard as oysters on the half shell." His name is Harry Jones and he is selling information. His information concerns Eddie Mars's wife, Mona. Mona Mars, it is generally agreed, disappeared about the same time as Rusty Regan and popular consensus has it that they left together. Mona's presumed relationship with Regan is also believed to be the primary impetus behind Eddie Mars's relationship with Vivian. But Harry Jones has information which suggests otherwise. Harry is a mouthpiece for Agnes, the bookstore clerk assumed to be allied with Joe Brody, and their association represents yet another fragmented piece of the local rackets organization at war with itself, a primary subplot. Agnes has recently seen Mona and is willing to divulge her whereabouts for sufficient cash.

Harry is too loyal to Agnes to convey the information himself and insists that Marlowe meet him later with the money, and he will take him to her. When Marlowe arrives at the appointed rendezvous, he discovers that Lash Canino, one of Eddie Mars's enforcers, has gotten there ahead of him and is trying to get Harry to tell him where Agnes is and what she knows. After Harry finally relents and gives him a false address to placate him, Canino offers whiskey to seal their "friendship." Harry dies quickly from the cyanide in the liquor as Marlowe stands by helplessly on the other side of the wall. He must wait until later for his chance at this embodiment of evil whom Harry had described simply as the "brown man": "Short, heavy set, brown hair, brown eyes, and always wears brown clothes and a brown hat. Even wears a brown suede raincoat. Drives a brown coupe. Everything brown for Mr. Canino."

With the aid of a chance phone call from Agnes, Marlowe makes contact with her, gets her information, and heads out into the hills where Mona Mars was spotted. The rain that has pervaded the book is now very heavy, and as Marlowe nears the appointed site, in his words, "Fate stage-managed the whole thing." His car skids off the slick roadway, and he finds himself near Art Huck's Garage, a hot-car processing establishment associated with Eddie Mars's rackets. Canino is there and, without much ado, Marlowe is overpowered and knocked unconscious.

When he comes to, Marlowe finds himself handcuffed, bound, and alone in a room with a woman. The woman is Mona Mars. Despite his condition, Marlowe manages to amuse her with his bright chatter. She is particularly amused that he thinks she is being held prisoner. She even removes her platinum wig, disclosing her bald head which she claims to have had shaved herself "to show Eddie I was willing to do what he wanted me to do—hide out. That he didn't need to have me guarded. I wouldn't let him down. I love him." Eventually, Marlowe's tireless talk manages to persuade her to help him escape rather than wait to see what his fate might be when Canino returns.

But before Marlowe can get well outside the house, Canino is back. When Canino goes inside, Marlowe starts his car and provokes him to fire from the window. Finally, the ruse draws Canino from the house and, with a bit of cooperation from Mona, Marlowe manages to get the drop on him. After Canino has fired six wild shots, Marlowe steps calmly from his hiding place, asks simply "Finished?" and fires four shots of his own into "the brown man," thus ending his reign of terror—and marking Marlowe's only killing in the novels.

Next morning, the sun is shining and Marlowe makes his way first to the police and then to General Sternwood to explain his findings and activities. General Sternwood is quite distressed that the police have been involved at all. Marlowe more or less apologizes by explaining that he has assumed from the beginning that there was more to the General's interest in the case than the simple matter of blackmail over debts. As he explains, "I was convinced that you put those Geiger notes up to me chiefly as a test, and that you were a little afraid Regan might somehow be involved in an attempt to blackmail you." Marlowe further elaborates that his disposition of the case has been based on the assumption that the police are not likely to overlook anything obvious in the course of their investigations. He sets himself distinctly apart from the more traditional detective of fiction:

> I'm not Sherlock Holmes or Philo Vance. I don't expect to go
> over ground the police have covered and pick up a broken pen
> point and build a case from it. . . . if they overlook any-
> thing . . . it's apt to be something looser and vaguer, like a
> man of Geiger's type sending you his evidence of debt and
> asking you to pay like a gentleman.

His explanations are sufficient to restore the General's confidence.
The old man allows that he is just "a sentimental old goat" and
tacitly admits that Regan has indeed been his primary concern all
along; he offers Marlowe $1,000 to "Find him. . . . Just find him."

On his way out of the house, Marlowe spots Carmen and returns the little pearl-handled pistol which he had taken away from
her in a scene where she tried to kill Joe Brody. "I brought you back
your artillery," he tells her. "I cleaned it and loaded it up. Take my
tip—don't shoot it at people, unless you get to be a better shot.
Remember?" Carmen's immediate reaction is, "Teach me to shoot."
And giggling in her strange way, she persuades him to drive her
to an old abandoned oil field on the family property. Here, amid
these reminders of the family fortune and its corruption, Marlowe
sets up a target. But as he is walking back from it, "she showed me
all her sharp little teeth and brought the gun up and started to
hiss. . . . 'Stand there, you son of a bitch,' she said." Marlowe laughs
and she fires at him—four times before he takes the gun from her. He
has anticipated the scene and loaded the gun with blanks. Carmen
makes a whistling sound in her throat and passes out.

After Marlowe has taken her home, he engages her older sister Vivian in conversation. From this encounter, then, we finally
gather enough details to begin to make sense of this curious and
deadly family tragedy. What we discover is that Carmen stands at
the center of the troubles. She suffers, among other things, from
epileptic attacks, as her behavior at the scene where Geiger was
killed, and the strange hissing, giggling noises she frequently utters
have already warned Marlowe.

When Regan disappeared, it was because Carmen killed him—
in the very same fashion in which she tried to kill Marlowe. Marlowe explains her actions, conjecturally, as a combination of her
epilepsy, adolescent lust, and the almost inevitable neurosis fos-
tered by the circumstances in which she was reared. As he tells

Vivian, "Night before last when I got home she was in my apartment. She'd kidded the manager into letting her in to wait for me. She was in my bed—naked. I threw her out on her ear. I guess maybe Regan did the same to her sometime. But you can't do that to Carmen."

Vivian admits that Carmen killed Regan and explains her own actions and motivations:

> She came home and told me about it just like a child. She's not normal. I knew the police would get it all out of her. In a little while she would even brag about it. And if dad knew, he would call them instantly and tell them the whole story. And sometime in that night he would die. It's not his dying—it's what he would be thinking just before he died. Rusty wasn't a bad fellow. I didn't love him. He was all right, I guess. He just didn't mean anything to me, one way or another, alive or dead, compared with keeping it from dad.

Vivian, of course, is not the type to approach reality head on; none of the Sternwoods are. As she perceived the situation, her only option was to try to cover up the matter, and the only person she knew powerful enough to help her do that was her gambling acquaintance Eddie Mars. Mars, of course, was only too glad to be of service; the incident clearly gave him leverage on the Sternwood fortune. Canino, no doubt, did the dirty work of stashing the body. But Mars's commitment to service went even further. When the police appeared to be coming too close to the truth, he had his own wife, Mona, hide out to make it appear that she and Regan had left together, thus giving the police a reasonable explanation for Regan's disappearance.

But Mars's greed was finally stronger than his patience. Geiger's whole blackmailing scheme appears, in fact, to have been a ploy sponsored by Mars. As Marlowe theorizes to Vivian:

> Eddie Mars was behind Geiger, protecting him and using him for a cat's-paw. Your father sent for me instead of paying up, which showed he wasn't scared about anything. Eddie Mars wanted to know that. He had something on you and he wanted to know if he had it on the General too. If he had, he could collect a lot of money in a hurry. If not, he would have

to wait until you got your share of the family fortune, and in
the meantime be satisfied with whatever spare cash he could
take away from you across the roulette table.

But this plan did not account for the unpredictable influence of
youthful passions. Owen Taylor, the Sternwood chauffeur, had his
own romantic interest in Carmen. He was violently affected by her
association with Geiger and when he discovered Geiger taking
nude pictures of her, pictures that were to be a part of the blackmail plot, he killed him. It was Taylor's fading footsteps that Marlowe heard in that first scene at Geiger's house. Geiger's death then
triggered a series of subplots. One of these involved his smut-lending
business. With Geiger gone, Joe Brody moved to take over the trade,
largely with the help of Agnes, Geiger's former assistant. This move
persuaded Carol Lundgren, Geiger's young homosexual roommate,
that Brody had been responsible for Geiger's death, so Lundgren
killed Brody. Harry Jones was then killed by Canino when Harry
tried to work a scheme with Agnes to sell information about Mona
to Marlowe. And Mars, without his front man, was forced into cover-
ing his own tracks.

Such is the mushrooming effect of one poorly conceived decision. Even an apparently well-intentioned act, such as Vivian's effort to cover up Carmen's murder of Regan, can become the initial
stone from which an expanding circle of evil radiates. Four deaths
result from Vivian's actions. Owen Taylor kills Geiger because he
does not approve of his relationship with Carmen. Carol Lundgren
kills Joe Brody because he thinks Brody killed Geiger. Canino kills
Harry Jones because he is getting too close to the truth and killing
is Canino's job. And Marlowe kills Canino.

But curiously enough, Marlowe must also share, at least par-
tially, in the blame for Harry's death. It was Marlowe, after all, who
mentioned to Mars that he was being followed; this tip called Mars's
attention to Harry's involvement in the story and led ultimately to
his death. Indeed, Marlowe must finally recognize himself to be more
subtly and pervasively involved in this very complex story than even
he at first imagined. Part of his realization comes when he asks the
butler, concerning the General, "What did this Regan fellow have
that bored into him so?" The answer he gets is, "Youth, sir. . . .

And the soldier's eye. . . . If I may say so, sir, not unlike yours." Understanding the similarity of Marlowe and Regan, at least in the General's eyes, is central to understanding the story. As readers, we, like Marlowe, begin to perceive that Vivian's decision to hide Carmen's murder of Regan may not, in fact, have been motivated solely by a desire to protect her sister or even to protect her ailing father. Rather, she may well have surmised that Regan was more important to the General than his own daughters. Thus, she may —rightly—have been more fearful of the unknown consequences of the discovery of the murder by her father than of opening herself to the blackmailing demands of Eddie Mars. Marlowe must feel more than a little uneasy as he realizes that he has been drawn into this family saga as a substitute for Regan, one surrogate son hired to ascertain the whereabouts of another, while the daughters slip ever further into the grips of gangsters.

But a sixth death in the book, that of Owen Taylor, may help illuminate our search for "first causes," for a place to lay ultimate responsibility for the chain of murders chronicled here. Shortly after the scene in which he kills Geiger, Taylor's car is found in the surf off Lido pier with him still in it. The hand throttle had been set halfway down, and he was apparently sapped before the car plunged through the barricades into the sea. But this case is never solved, although Joe Brody is a prime suspect. When the first film version of *The Big Sleep* was being prepared, the screenwriters even sent a query to Chandler: "Who killed Owen Taylor?" Chandler's response was a simple "I don't know."

The incident is important because it calls attention to Chandler's general distaste for the typical demand that detective stories should tie up every loose end. Furthermore, it underscores his deep-seated aversion to strictly rational explanations for human actions. If we look closely at Vivian's decision to cover Carmen's deadly act, for example, we simply can not devise a purely rational account of it. Given the implied strife between the two sisters, Vivian's less-than-loving relationship with her father, and the fact that Carmen's victim was her own husband (even if she did not love him), Vivian's act simply can not be circumscribed within rational bounds. Nevertheless, given Vivian's character, her environment, and an emotionally-charged situation, we can readily *believe* that she might make such a decision. The deeper we penetrate the motives of Chandler's characters, the deeper we find the morass of human passion and unpredictability.

But if Chandler is not interested in constructing neatly rational puzzles, what exactly is he up to here? We can glean at least a partial answer to this perplexing question from a close examination of the opening scene and some related passages. When Marlowe first comes to call on the Sternwood millions, his attention is arrested by a curious drama in glass:

> Over the entrance doors, which would have let in a troop of Indian elephants, there was a broad stained-glass panel showing a knight in dark armor rescuing a lady who was tied to a tree and didn't have any clothes on but some very long and convenient hair. The knight had pushed the vizor of his helmet back to be sociable, and he was fiddling with the knots on the ropes that tied the lady to the tree and not getting anywhere. I stood there and thought that if I lived in the house, I would sooner or later have to climb up there and help him. He didn't seem to be really trying.

Critics have often complained that Chandler was overly concerned with sentimentalism and the tropes of the chivalric romance; the kind of elements on which this glass panel focuses. But even a cursory look at Chandler's overt references to the romance and knight-errantry within the novel, as here, indicates a decided touch of irony in his treatment of the subject. Indeed, *The Big Sleep* might be read as a chronicle of the *failure* of romance. In the midst of one of his confrontations with Carmen, for example, Marlowe turns to his chess board for distraction. He makes a move with a knight, then retracts it and comments, "the move with the knight was wrong. I put it back where I had moved it from. Knights had no meaning in this game. It wasn't a game for knights." And near the end of the book, he comments again on the knight in the stained-glass window saying, he "still wasn't getting anywhere untying the naked damsel from the tree."

Carmen, of course, *is* the naked damsel in distress in this book, and finally we and Marlowe must ask ourselves if he has really been any more successful in aiding her than has the knight in armor trapped forever in the glass. And we must agree that he has not.

About all that can be said for Marlowe here as the "romantic hero" is that he does, at least, keep Carmen from killing anyone else while he is on the scene. And he keeps her from being killed or from facing the harsh justice of the legal system—rather, he advises Vivian to "take her away. . . . Hell, she might even get herself cured, you know. It's been done." But he has been totally ineffectual in penetrating the mystery of this family and its seemingly inexorable involvement with the world of crime. He has achieved no ennobling resolution. He has had no success in getting at the heart of this saga which is finally the story of two women, two sisters, Carmen and Vivian, and the last days of a dying old patriarch. Marlowe's understanding is hardly less limited than Vivian's, and she can not bear to probe her actions very deeply:

> I knew Eddie Mars would bleed me white, but I didn't care. I had to have help and I could only get it from somebody like him. . . . There have been times when I hardly believed it all myself. And other times when I had to get drunk quickly—whatever time of day it was. Awfully damn quickly.

In Vivian's reluctance to face her relation to evil squarely, Chandler reminds us all of the limits of our ability to approach and comprehend the truth. Even if we still possess the idealistic, romantic sensibilities that can drive us to noble actions, the consequences, like the motives, are never really unadulterated. And finally, like Marlowe, we are impotent to untie the knots of our lives. He tries, like Vivian, simply to avoid seeing, to deaden his sensibilities; in the book's last paragraph he "stopped at a bar and had a couple of double Scotches." But, as he recognizes, "they didn't do me any good." Avoiding complexity does not resolve it.

As he walks out of the Sternwood house for the last time, Marlowe comments: "Outside, the bright gardens had a haunted look, as though small wild eyes were watching me from behind the bushes, as though the sunshine itself had a mysterious something in its light." At the end, there is still mystery—the mystery of the human condition, of life and death in a world of fate and chance and evil.

Marlowe tries to pass it off with his remark, "What did it matter where you lay once you were dead? . . . You were dead, you were sleeping the big sleep, you were not bothered by things like that." But the thought does not satisfy him. This depressed, perplexed man is a sharp contrast to the cocky, well-dressed detective who first called on the Sternwoods. A general uneasiness pervades his mood and the close of the story. Whatever resolution the novel offers is only in the most simplistic sense of knowing who killed whom—and even that information (as in the case of Owen Taylor) is limited. It is a story thoroughly lacking in satisfying explanations for why things happened as they did. But that is not necessarily a criticism of Chandler's plotting; it is perhaps instead an articulation of his basic point.

*Farewell, My Lovely* (1940) continues to elaborate many of the basic themes established in *The Big Sleep*. It seeks simple, straightforward explanations for the plot's sinister actions but must settle, finally, for conjecture on the multiplicity of possible motivations behind its characters' deeds. Sentimentalism and the quest of the romantic knight are again mocked, and Marlowe, again, undergoes an experience of recognition which embodies the book's essential message. The controlling notion which is new to this plot involves what appears at first to be some sort of general conspiracy aimed at Marlowe's elimination.

As the story opens, we see Marlowe in a scene which epitomizes his character and his place in the world. He is wandering the streets, working rather casually on a missing persons case when he becomes absorbed by events happening around him. As he says, "Nothing made it my business except curiosity." That curiosity draws his attention, specifically, to a man, "a big man but not more than six feet five inches tall and not wider than a beer truck. . . . about as inconspicuous as a tarantula on a slice of angel food," and once involved Marlowe can not turn away from the story until he has gained some understanding of it.

The big man is registering his apparent displeasure with the changes in the neighborhood by tossing the regular black patrons of one of the clubs into the street. Captivated by the scene, Marlowe soon finds himself being dragged inside and regaled with the big man's story. Moose Malloy, as he is known, is looking for "Little Velma" whom he hasn't seen since he went to prison on bank robbery charges eight years earlier. Although he hasn't heard from her for the last six of those years, he is convinced that "she'll have a reason" and that his love will ultimately transcend whatever else may have happened in the meanwhile. Completely oblivious to the fact that the neighborhood is changing from white to black (partly accounting for his conspicuousness), Moose has come looking for Velma at this club because she used to sing here. Having recounted this much, Moose insists on barging into the back office of Mr. Montgomery, the manager, to pursue his investigation. Marlowe soon hears a "dull flat sound" that proves to be the book's first murder. As Moose makes his exit, we sense that Marlowe has already been, in some sense, trapped by these events. He simply can't resist picking up the threads of Moose's rather ineptly begun investigation. In short order, he locates Jessie Florian, wife of the former owner of the club where "Little Velma" once sang. A dilapidated old drunk living in a dilapidated old house, Mrs. Florian says Velma is dead. But her attempt to keep Velma's photo from Marlowe leaves him wondering if she is trying to hide something, afraid of Moose, or simply disapproving of him and his style.

Back at his office, Marlowe is temporarily distracted by a paying customer. The unexpected caller is Lindsay Marriott who wants Marlowe to accompany him at the transfer of $8,000, supposedly a ransom for a jade necklace stolen from a friend of Marriott's. At the appointed rendezvous, an isolated spot in Purissima Canyon, Marlowe's suspicions are aroused, and he leaves Marriott alone in the car to investigate. Suddenly a club swishes through the darkness; when Marlowe comes to, muttering to himself, someone with a flashlight—and a gun—is holding him at bay. The voice behind the light and gun is feminine, but it is unperturbed by Marlowe's snarling "Put it up—or I'll blow it out of your hand!" The voice is that of Anne Riordan. Her presence is not explained. Understandably, she takes no chances with Marlowe because she has already discovered that Lin Marriott is dead.

But Marlowe's "nice sense of humor—like a morgue attendant" and his own less-than-perfect physical condition persuade her of his trustworthiness, and together they examine the body. Among

Marriott's personal possessions, they find three marijuana cigarettes, or "jujus" as Riordan calls them. Resisting her further offers of assistance, Marlowe leaves to confront the police alone.

The following morning, Anne Riordan is waiting for Marlowe when he arrives at his office. And once again in the story, Marlowe finds himself complementing another investigator's work; Riordan, whose father was a cop (a detail which explains her toughness with Marlowe the night before), has already opened a few leads in the case. She has talked to Detective Lieutenant Randall, the man in charge of the case, and found out about the jade necklace at the center of the Marriott plot, information which Marlowe withheld from her the previous evening. From a jeweler she has discovered the owner of the necklace, Mrs. Lewin Lockridge Grayle, and from a newspaper society editor she has already gathered details about the owner's private life. She has even acquired a photograph of Mrs. Grayle. Marlowe says of it, "It was a blonde. A blonde to make a bishop kick a hole in a stained-glass window." Riordan has even arranged a business appointment for Marlowe with Mrs. Grayle. And before she leaves, she admits to having taken the jujus off Marriott the night before. In her words, "I thought it was kind of mean for the poor man to be found dead with marijuana cigarettes in his pocket."

Left alone with the jujus, Marlowe cuts one open to inspect its contents and finds, curiously, a calling card rolled inside—the card of Jules Amthor, Psychic Consultant. A call from Lt. Randall warns Marlowe to stay off the case, but his curiosity is still in command, and he calls Amthor.

While arranging to meet this Amthor character, Marlowe checks with a friend who works with a title company and discovers that Jessie Florian's house has been recently refinanced by a man named Lindsay Marriott. Suddenly, there is a connection, Lindsay Marriott, between the jade necklace case and the Moose Malloy case, and the two stories begin to mesh.

This new information stirs Marlowe to pay another visit to Jessie Florian. On the way, he calls on a neighbor, Mrs. Morrison, who confirms that a man meeting Moose Malloy's description has visited Mrs. Florian and that she receives a letter by registered mail on the first of every month, a letter presumed by Marlowe to be some kind of payoff. Mrs. Florian herself explains the Marriott connection by saying, "I used to work for him. . . . I used to be a servant in his family. He kind of takes care of me a little."

Back at his office, the phone rings and it is Mrs. Grayle's butler requesting a meeting with Marlowe "as soon as convenient." When the meeting occurs, Mrs. Grayle's side of the necklace theft story strongly implicates Marriott. His choice of route on the night they were stopped and the necklace taken suggests the possibility that he was collaborating with the hold-up men. And besides, as she explains, "Lin Marriott was a high-class blackmailer, of course. That's obvious. He lived on women." His hold over Mrs. Grayle appears to have resulted from his having taken some nude photographs of her when she "got a little tight at his house once and passed out."

But our confidence in Mrs. Grayle as a reliable witness is short-lived. Within moments, she has made a heavy-handed attempt to seduce Marlowe, virtually in front of her aging husband, and has made arrangements for a further rendezvous at the Belvedere Club, an establishment operated by the local gambling rackets boss, Laird Brunette.

In the course of Marlowe's conversation with Mrs. Grayle, she more or less offers to employ him to retrieve her necklace, but a financial agreement is never formalized. Shortly after, in a conversation with Anne Riordan, Marlowe has decided "there's nothing for me in it" and is worrying that "I've got to watch my step. This Grayle packs a lot of dough in his pants. And law is where you buy it in this town. Look at the funny way the cops are acting. No build-up, no newspaper handout. . . . Nothing but silence and warnings to me to lay off. I don't like it at all."

Marlowe is aware of his own vulnerability in the face of the powers at work here. (Chandler once considered calling this novel *Law Is Where You Buy It.*) And he hardly has a client, after all. But if he has any serious thoughts about quitting the case, events and his own undying curiosity refuse to allow it.

When he gets back to his office, a Hollywood Indian named Second Planting has arrived as an emissary from Jules Amthor and insists on accompanying Marlowe to visit the psychic. Amthor himself, we soon find, is a thin, tall, straight man with skin "as fresh as a rose petal" who "might have been thirty-five or sixty-five" and who has the "depthless eyes of the somnambulist." He is the type

who works with a white globe on a white table in a room draped
in black velvet. At first, he is evasive in response to Marlowe's questions. But when Marlowe goes so far as to suggest that Marriott was
the "finger man for a jewel mob" which needed someone, perhaps
Amthor, with the knowledge of the habits of wealthy women as a
coordinator, Amthor professes to be "slightly disgusted" by the
suggestion, and the lights go out.

A brief brawl between Second Planting and Marlowe ensues,
and Marlowe does not fare well. Without explanation, he is turned
over to a couple of Bay City policemen, marking the beginning
of one of the novel's extended jokes. One of the cops has a habit
of repeating things after Marlowe says them and provokes him to
retort: "Listen, Hemingway, don't repeat everything I say." When
the cop finally asks, "Who is this Hemingway person at all?" Marlowe replies: "A guy that keeps saying the same thing over and
over until you begin to believe it must be good." Such wit in the
face of adversity is one of Marlowe's distinguishing characteristics,
a technique which often serves to throw his foes off stride just
enough for him to retaliate. And such internal mocking of a man
who was, in fact, one of his literary mentors, is Chandler's way of
paying his respects while, at the same time, calling into question
the whole literary enterprise of which he is himself a part. The
joke also serves, of course, as comic relief in the midst of this
macabre tale where there is little to laugh about.

Certainly, there is little humor in the treatment Marlowe receives at the hands of these suburban cops. Without warning or
provocation, he is sapped—again—and wakes up in a smoke-filled,
sparsely furnished, guarded room which he has never seen before.
His erratic behavior, disjointed thoughts, and the pin pricks on
his arm suggest that he has been subdued by powerful drugs. By
yelling "Fire," he attracts a guard to his room, overcomes him, and
escapes. While roaming about this new "prison," he notices Moose
Malloy reading the newspaper and apparently enjoying himself in
one of the rooms.

Further along the corridor, Marlowe comes upon the office of
the establishment and stumbles in to confront its proprietor, Dr.
Sonderborg. Sonderborg claims that Marlowe was "properly committed by an officer of the law" but such platitudes are hardly
enlightening. Wielding a gun which he has taken from Dr. Sonder-

borg's desk, Marlowe makes good his escape, realizes he is in the neighborhood where Anne Riordan lives, and goes to her house.

Riordan provides him with enough food and black coffee to restore his health and he lays out most of the story for her. Events have persuaded him that it is a more complicated matter than just Amthor running a jewelry mob. But again he refuses further assistance from Riordan—insults her in fact—and insists on going home to his "homely smell, a smell of dust and tobacco smoke, the smell of a world where men live, and keep on living." The scene calls attention to Marlowe's deep-seated alienation and his difficulty in trusting anyone.

The following morning Lieutenant Randall pays a call on Marlowe, and together they thrash out the theory that Marriott's death was engineered by the jewel mob for whom he was presumably working. Randall has also come across the deed to Jessie Florian's house in Marriott's safe deposit box, and, together, he and Marlowe set out to visit her with the hope of shedding more light on that relationship. But they are too late. Jessie Florian is dead of strangulation, and the spacing of the finger marks on her neck suggests a killer the size of Moose Malloy.

Back at City Hall, Randall and Marlowe deduce that Malloy "probably didn't mean to kill her. . . . He's just too strong." Randall has, in fact, uncovered a motive for Malloy's violence toward Jessie Florian. When Malloy was arrested eight years ago on the bank robbery charge, he was picked up at Florian's, as the club was then called. A thousand-dollar reward was paid, and Malloy likely figured that the Florians got at least a part of the money or knew who did. As Randall suggests, "maybe he was just trying to shake it out of her."

Despite Randall's further requests that Marlowe leave the Marriott and Malloy cases to the police, Marlowe is shortly taking matters into his own hands again and calling on the Chief of Police of Bay City, John Wax. By playing upon his association with the Grayles and the political power associated with their fortune, he quickly has the Chief in a cooperative mood—although the Chief insists that "Trouble . . . is something our little city don't know much about."

Marlowe proceeds to tell about his experience with Amthor and the two Bay City cops, Galbraith (Hemingway) and Blane.

But he says he figures the mistake was a natural one, and he only wants "to square myself with Amthor and I want your man Galbraith to help me do it."

When he gets Galbraith alone, Marlowe admits that the information he's really after concerns the reasons for his being placed at Sonderborg's and kept there. Marlowe is convinced that the conspiracy against him is real. Galbraith's explanation is simply that "we are friends with this swami guy [Amthor] and we kind of keep people from bothering him." He says further that old cops, like Blane, just "get sap hungry once in a while" and that when Marlowe "dropped like a sack of cement, I told Blane plenty. Then we run you over to Sonderborg's place on account of it was a little closer and he was a nice guy and would take care of you." He claims Amthor knew nothing about their transfer of Marlowe to Sonderborg's, and says he has no idea why Sonderborg detained him for forty-eight hours.

In the course of their conversation, Galbraith explains to Marlowe what's wrong with the country and offers some insight into his own character: "A guy can't stay honest if he wants to. . . . He gets chiseled out of his pants if he does. You gotta play the game dirty or you don't eat." Galbraith is just a "little man" trapped within a system over which he has no control. In that system, honesty is synonymous with gullibility and survival is contingent upon one's ability to adapt. As he puts it, in a bit of tangled syntax, "They get you where they have you do what is told them or else." Responsibility recedes into the haze of confused pronouns. Galbraith is just a man like many others, "getting by," doing what has to be done to maintain what little autonomy and security he can lay hold of. When he and Marlowe arrive at Sonderborg's, the place appears deserted. Moose Malloy, we assume, is on the lam again.

Marlowe is next seen resting in a cheap waterfront hotel, waiting for the darkness to provide him the opportunity to play another hunch. This one concerns the two gambling ships operated by rackets boss Brunette just outside the three-mile limit. He first tries boarding one of the ships via the water taxi, along with all the other gamblers, lovers, and tourists. But a guard on the landing refuses him entry because of the gun he is rather too obviously carrying in his shoulder holster.

Back on the dock, Marlowe encounters "a big redheaded roughneck" whose own curiosity draws him to Marlowe's plight. When Marlowe asks, "What's *your* racket?," he responds, "A dollar here, a dollar there. I was on the cops once. They broke me." A friendship is struck (a friendship which certain critics have interpreted as homosexual—see Chapter 6), and Red offers to assist Marlowe in boarding one of the ships through a loading port which he knows to be unlocked.

On the ride out, Red offers his own theorizing on the state of the world. As he sees it:

> These racketeers are a new type. . . . Big-mouthed police commissioners on the radio yell that they're all yellow rats, that they'll kill women and babies and howl for mercy if they see a police uniform. They ought to know better than to try to sell the public that stuff. There's yellow cops and there's yellow torpedoes—but damn few of either. And as for the top men, like Brunette—they didn't get there by murdering people. They got there by guts and brains—and they don't have the group courage the cops have either. But above all they're business men. What they do is for money.

With Red's help, Marlowe gets aboard the ship, manages to get the drop on a couple of Brunette's underlings in what he mockingly calls "a bum scene," and herds them into Brunette's office.

Brunette is most interested in learning how Marlowe managed to get on his ship. Marlowe's cooperation on that point persuades Brunette to be at least marginally cooperative in assisting him. Marlowe mentions Sonderborg, suggests that he was running a hideout for "hot boys," and that "he couldn't do that without connections. I don't think he could do it without you." Brunette suggests "You're simple. . . . Supposing I wanted to hide him, why should I take the risk out here? . . . The world is full of places a crook can hide. If he has money. Could you think of a better idea?"

The stalemate ends with Brunette agreeing to get a message to Moose Malloy if he can, but he still insists he knows nothing about him. The message which Marlowe leaves scrawled across the back of one of his business cards is an ambiguous, "It means nothing to me."

When Marlowe makes it home later that evening, he phones Mrs. Grayle and invites her by to "show you my etching." But in the interim, he falls asleep exhausted. A movement in the room wakes him. It is Moose Malloy; he has already gotten the message. But before they have much chance to talk, Mrs. Grayle is at the door. Marlowe sends Moose into another room. The conversation between Marlowe and Mrs. Grayle turns to murder, and Marlowe strings together for her his long list of circumstantial evidence which ultimately accuses her of having killed Lindsay Marriott.

Mrs. Grayle pulls a gun. Moose Malloy steps from the other room. " 'I thought I knew that voice,' he said. 'I listened to that voice for eight years—all I could remember of it. I kind of liked your hair red, though. Hiya, babe. Long time no see.' " Mrs. Grayle turns the gun on Malloy, empties it into his stomach and flees.

Without his dream to live for, Malloy dies in the night. Mrs. Grayle is found three months later in Baltimore where a local detective recognizes her as the singer in a nightclub. But when he tries to arrest her, she shoots him, turns the gun on herself and, in Detective Randall's words, "Shot herself clean through the heart—twice" in a violent farewell.

*Farewell, My Lovely* is a book which raises many questions about the relationships between people and the forces of good and evil at loose in the world. In characteristic Chandler fashion, several of these are never really answered, but those that are and those about which answers are hinted outline for us the motivations which propel this plot and, by extension, which propel society.

Initially, the tale, with its seemingly unrelated strands, appears to involve some grand conspiracy to silence Marlowe. Given his near encounter with death in the scene where Marriott is murdered, his meeting with Amthor and Second Planting, the beating he suffers at the hands of the Bay City police, the "dope cure" he undergoes at Sonderborg's establishment, and an implied but nebulous connection between Mrs. Grayle and rackets boss Brunette, it is easy to understand why Marlowe keeps searching for a single explanation that would tie all these events together.

The jewelry theft ring preying on rich women appears to be the most likely common denominator. Detective Lieutenant Randall lends credibility to this theory by observing that "This jewel gang has been working in Hollywood and around for a good ten years to my knowledge." And at least two reasonable explanations suggest that Marriott's death was at the hands of such a gang. Marlowe's first idea is that "Killing Marriott was a dumb mistake. . . . What must have happened was that some gowed-up run they took along for a gun-holder lost his head. Marriott made a false move and some punk beat him down and it was done so quickly nothing could be done to prevent it." Later, when Marlowe becomes convinced that Marriott may well have been "the finger man for the jewel mob" he theorizes that "they used him up. His usefulness was exhausted. It was about time for him to get talked about a little. . . . But you don't quit in those rackets and you don't get your time. So this last holdup was just that for him—the last."

The actions of Amthor, Sonderborg, the Bay City cops, and even of Brunette and Mrs. Grayle all support the idea of a great conspiracy. But slowly, we amass evidence of other, more private, motivations behind each of these actions. Finally, we realize with Marlowe that the crime pervading society is not the result of general collusion, but is instead simply a compilation of individual rackets and petty people each protecting his or her own picayunish scheme.

Amthor, for example, explains quite openly to Marlowe that he knows himself to be "a quack. . . . in danger at all times—from people like you. I merely wish to estimate the danger before dealing with it." Similarly, Sonderborg is just a man with "a small time racket. A peanut grift." He hides criminals and, apparently, peddles dope. His rigid handling of Marlowe is evidently a result of his uncertainty about why Marlowe was brought to him in the first place: "he might have thought putting me in there was a police gag."

The cops, of course, have already explained their actions in rather obvious, human terms. Amthor was just "a friend" they were helping out, Blane just got "sap hungry," and Sonderborg's just happened to be the nearest place where they knew Marlowe would be "taken care of."

In the same way, Brunette muses ironically near the end of the story about, "The things I do. . . . I run towns, I elect mayors, I corrupt police, I peddle dope, I hide out crooks, I heist old women strangled with pearls. What a lot of time I have." Clearly, Brunette is not as innocent as his philosophic dissembling would have us believe, but there is also little reason to believe that he is at the head of a monolithic plot to corrupt the local community. As Red rightly acknowledged, Brunette is, in some sense, just a "business man."

Rather than chronicling a great conspiracy, this story hangs by a much more human thread. It is, indeed, as many human tales are, a love story. Eight years ago, Moose Malloy was imprisoned for bank robbery. Upon his release, his sole motivation was to find the woman he loved, Velma. But Velma had changed her name and hair color, and she had a new lifestyle to protect and the money with which to protect it. As Marlowe has it figured, Jessie Florian had at least enough knowledge of her past to extort support payments, but Marriott, the man Velma employed to deal with Jessie, obviously had a greater knowledge of her delicate position. When Moose got out of jail and he and a private dick (Marlowe) started nosing around, Marriott suddenly became a menace. He was the boy who knew too much and who could be made to talk too easily. He was the weak link that Velma had to silence.

Chandler sharpens the irony of this explanation by comparing Marriott's plight to that of the second murderer in Shakespeare's *King Richard III*. Marlowe quips that like Marriott, "the fellow . . . had certain dregs of conscience, but still wanted the money, and in the end didn't do the job at all because he couldn't make up his mind. Such murderers are very dangerous. They have to be removed—sometimes with blackjacks." (The centrality of Marriott and his uncertain position are underscored by another of Chandler's alternative titles for this novel, *The Second Murderer*.)

But the major irony pervading this book evolves from the fact that love is at its root. Moose loved Velma, and his unrelenting search for her generated this legacy of death. As Marlowe says, "That's what makes it funny, tragic-funny." As in *The Big Sleep*, evil and death have again been spawned by an essentially pure, if naive, motive. And, again, the notion of the romantic quest is thoroughly mocked. Velma is here transformed (mostly by money) into a "grail," the object of the knight's traditional quest. But Moose Malloy, a bumbling knight at best, finds that his search for the lovely, if not holy, Mrs. "Grayle" only leads to death—at her hands.

Moreover, at the end of the book, Chandler offers a comment on sentimentality, a quality associated with romanticism and of

which he is often accused. Trying to explain Velma's suicide, Marlowe argues that it was perhaps a generous gesture, an effort to
spare her aging husband the embarrassment of a trial, to protect
"an old man who had loved not wisely, but too well." Randall
objects, "That's just sentimental," but Marlowe replies, "Sure. It
sounded like that when I said it. Probably all a mistake anyway.
So long. Did my pink bug ever get back up here?"

The reference to the pink bug underscores Marlowe's, and
Chandler's, recognition of the essentially romantic, perhaps futile,
quality of much of human activity. The pink bug first appeared in
Randall's office. It captured Marlowe's attention:

> A shiny black bug with a pink head and pink spots on it
> crawled slowly along . . . and waved a couple of feelers around,
> as if testing the breeze for a takeoff. . . . The bug reached the
> end of Randall's desk and marched straight off into the air. It
> fell on its back on the floor, waved a few thin worn legs in the
> air feebly and then played dead. Nobody cared, so it began
> waving the legs again and finally struggled over on its face. It
> trundled slowly off into a corner towards nothing, going
> nowhere.

Marlowe identifies with this solitary, implacable creature and its
steadfast devotion to a seemingly pointless mission. He watches the
bug throughout his conversation with Randall. At its end, Randall
says, "I think Jessie Florian was Marriott's lucky piece. As long as
he took care of her, nothing would happen to him." Marlowe responds by picking up the bug and declaring, "This room is eighteen
floors above ground. And this little bug climbs all the way up here
just to make a friend. Me. *My* luck piece." Much to Randall's as-
tonishment, he then carries the bug down on the elevator, deposits
it in a flower bed and wonders on the way home "how long it
would take him to make the Homicide Bureau again."

Thus, Marlowe's final comment in the book ("Did my pink
bug ever get back up here?") acknowledges both the simplicity
and the pervasiveness of such sentimentality. While he recognizes
that the sentiments implicit in human actions can not withstand
the cold light of reason and logic, neither can he avoid identifying
with them. He knows that he himself, like the little pink bug, will

likely be marching straight off into thin air or trundling off into corners toward nothing, going nowhere, beating his head against immovable walls the very next time he takes on a case.

Likewise, the failure of Moose Malloy's romantic quest will do nothing to hinder similar fated missions by others in the future. The impulses—romantic or sentimental—it appears, may not meet the rigorous tests of the mind's higher faculties, and may engender disastrous ends, but they nonetheless persist as basic motivators, and perhaps essential flaws, of the human condition.

As Chandler was putting the final touches on *The High Window* (1942), he wrote his publisher:

> I'm afraid the book is not going to be any good to you. No action, no likeable characters, no nothing. The detective does nothing. . . . About all I can say by way of extenuation is that I tried my best and seemed to have to get the thing out of my system. I suppose I would have kept tinkering at it indefinitely otherwise.

His anticipation of the criticism was accurate; many observers have, in fact, commented on the book's lack of "likeable characters." Russell Davies has argued that, "By giving almost all the characters a share of it, Chandler has made misanthropy a semi-conscious theme of *The High Window,* which probably accounts for its relative failure at the deeper levels of interest."

But a weakness even closer to its surface lies in the fact that *The High Window* is two stories that are insufficiently woven together. One story involves an older woman (Mrs. Elizabeth Bright Murdock), her young, neurotic secretary (Merle Davis), and a blackmail scheme which stems from the questionable circumstances surrounding the death of Mrs. Murdock's first husband eight years in the past. The second story concerns the theft and counterfeiting of an antique gold coin, the Brashear Doubloon, the original of which has disappeared from Mrs. Murdock's collection. (Initially, Chandler wanted to call this book *The Brashear Doubloon* but was dissuaded by his publisher who was afraid the public might pronounce Brashear *brassiere.*)

The doubloon story occupies by far the greater portion of the book and of Marlowe's time. But finally the motive behind the doubloon counterfeiting is revealed to be strictly a desire for quick profit. Simple greed—a powerful part of the human psyche to be sure—is just not as engrossing as the subtler shades of trust, mistrust, love, power, and mental derangement that Chandler handled so skillfully in the first two novels. While the plot does explore such motivations to a degree, its power is diminished by the secondary status given to the more intriguing relationship between Mrs. Murdock and Miss Davis. Moreover, Chandler's efforts to link these plots are unconvincing. Even though the man behind the counterfeiting, Vannier, is also Mrs. Murdock's blackmailer, we rarely encounter him, and the crucial bridge between the two stories is never adequately realized.

But neither is *The High Window* a complete failure. To consider it so would be to fall into the trap of reading Chandler strictly for plot, an approach against which he cautioned many times.

What success the novel achieves is precisely in its examination of its two central female characters. Mrs. Murdock is a woman with "a lot of face and chin. She had pewter-colored hair set in a ruthless permanent, a hard beak and large moist eyes with the sympathetic expressions of wet stones." She reclines magisterially in a darkened room where she sips port and dispatches orders. As Marlowe's eyes become accustomed to its dim light, he realizes that the room is, prophetically, "a sort of sun porch that had been allowed to get completely overgrown outside." Her companion, Miss Davis, is characterized as "pale with a sort of natural paleness. . . . and coarse-grained coppery blond hair [that] was not ugly in itself, but it was drawn back so tightly over her narrow head that it almost lost the effect of being hair at all. . . . The whole face had a sort of off-key neurotic charm that only needed some clever makeup to be striking." She seems to perceive her role as protecting Mrs. Murdock from the outside world while submitting to her every whim, or, in her words, "doing what I'm told." She hides a small Colt automatic in her desk.

Essentially, we discover that Miss Davis' weak self-esteem and propensity to guilt have been so manipulated by Mrs. Murdock that Miss Davis assumes herself responsible for the death of Mrs. Murdock's husband. Her guilt is reinforced by the credibility of her motive; the husband, Horace Bright, had made sexual advances toward her, advances which frightened and repulsed her. Her devotion to Mrs. Murdock is in appreciation of Mrs. Murdock's protection of her "secret."

Chandler, characteristically, gives short space and an ironic tone to psychological explanations of behavior, but he does give them, and the explanations offer some insight into this curious pair. Dr. Carl Moss theorizes that the emotional shock of Mr. Bright's death would likely have driven Miss Davis to attempt to make "the subconscious attempt to escape back to childhood. If Mrs. Murdock scolds her a good deal, but not too much, that would increase the tendency. Identification of childhood subordination with childhood protection." Marlowe's reaction to such theorizing is to growl, "Do we have to go into that stuff?" But the explanation is there nonetheless, and we can easily believe that a young woman of Miss Davis' impressionable constitution might well exhibit regressive, submissive behavior at the hands of such a tyrannizing figure as Mrs. Murdock.

Their relationship, then, is largely a study of the use and abuse of power. The shakiest part of such an explanation concerns Mrs. Murdock's motivations. Marlowe's only conjecture on the matter comes when he tells Merle that she has been manipulated "with care, deliberation and the sort of quiet ruthlessness you only find in a certain kind of woman dealing with another woman. . . . She's cold, bitter, unscrupulous and she used you without mercy, or pity, as insurance, in case Vannier ever blew his top. You were just a scapegoat to her." How she serves as "insurance," exactly, is never made clear. That Vannier's photographic evidence about the murder of Horace Bright clearly indicates that Merle was *not* responsible would seem to negate her value as a "scapegoat." The lack of clear-cut motivations on this point might suggest a weakness in Chandler's plotting. But it might also indicate another case where complicated human interactions transcend a search for strictly logical explanations.

Such insight as is available concerning Mrs. Murdock's motivations is oblique. It is there to be inferred from her appearance, from her self-indulgences, from her dictatorial arrogance, from her cheating at solitaire, and from the symbolic decadence of the overgrown sun porch from which she rules her petty and crumbling fiefdom. She is an embodiment of selfishness in the novel, capable of using others, even her own son Leslie, to spiteful and petty ends.

That son, "a slim tall self-satisfied looking number," who smokes cigarettes through a long black cigarette holder while wearing white pigskin gloves, is a vital link between the book's two main threads. With his "smile of a bored aristocrat," he is the perfect pawn of both his mother's tyranny and the professional criminals who are, again, a shadow of the wealthy here, as they were in the first two novels. But the professional criminals in this book are not merely disorganized; they are bunglers. Their grand scheme to milk a fortune from the counterfeiting of the Brashear doubloon is sabotaged by a well-informed coin dealer and a well-intentioned, if amateurish, young private detective, George Anson Phillips.

Marlowe, in his methodical manner, keeps trying to make sense of it all and to make the other characters make sense of it for themselves. But his mission proves futile. After Leslie admits to killing Vannier but pleads that it was accidental, for example, Marlowe's frustration explodes:

> Why spoil it? . . . Why not make it a nice clean honest murder? . . . You say it was an accident. Okay, it was an accident. I wasn't a witness. I haven't any proof either way. I've been working for your mother and whatever right to my silence that gives her, she can have. I don't like her, I don't like you, I don't like this house. I didn't particularly like your wife. But I like Merle. She's kind of silly and morbid, but she's kind of sweet too.

Merle, for her part, remains oblivious to the end regarding her treatment at the hands of Mrs. Murdock. Marlowe's speech about her being used as a scapegoat elicits only, "Mrs. Murdock has been wonderful to me, always. . . . you shouldn't say such awful things about people." Even when he shows her the photographic proof of how the murder of Horace Bright occurred, Merle responds, "You must never show this to Mrs. Murdock. It would upset her terribly." Marlowe is exasperated. His solution for Merle is to take her home to her parents in Wichita, Kansas, where domesticity appears to have ambiguous effects. We last see her rolling pie crust, kissing Marlowe goodbye, then running back into the house crying. Whether her tears are of joy or sorrow is not at all discernible. Marlowe's comment here—"I had a funny feeling as I saw the house disappear, as though I had written a poem and it was very good and I had lost it and would never remember it again"—calls attention to his own ambiguous reaction to these events. He feels that he has come very close to some essential understanding of human nature, the kind of thing best expressed in poetry, but in the end it has slipped away from him.

But *blame*, finally, is a major theme of this book. One of the subjects on which the book attempts to make a statement—and which contributes to Marlowe's incomplete understanding—is that of blame. When he gets Merle home to Wichita, Marlowe says of her parents, "they blamed themselves a lot, and I let them do it." Merle, of course, has been blaming herself for the death of Horace Bright for eight years. And when Louis Vannier finally meets his death, there are three characters who confess to his murder—all despite some rather impressive clues that he died by suicide. Apparently, accepting blame allows these characters the illusion of having accepted responsibility. But, such uncritical acquiescence to blame, we are reminded, stems from the same "identification of childhood subordination with childhood protection" from which Merle has been suffering for most of her life. It is an infantile approach to the world and is finally self-destructive.

Once again, we look to Marlowe and the toll which these revelations take on his own sensibilities for clues to the novel's meaning. When Merle persists in believing that Mrs. Murdock is "really awfully kind" despite his detailing of her tyranny, Marlowe exits to the kitchen for a quick drink. But, in a statement that echoes the end of *The Big Sleep*, he says, "It didn't do me any good. It just made me want to climb up the wall and gnaw my way across the ceiling." And after the trip to Wichita and a final meeting with Lieutenant Breeze that ties some of the story's loose ends together, he says:

> I went home and put my old house clothes on and set the chessmen out and mixed a drink and played over another Capablanca. It went fifty-nine moves. Beautiful cold remorseless chess, almost creepy in its silent implacability.

When it was done I listened at the open window for a while and smelled the night. Then I carried my glass out to the kitchen and rinsed it and filled it with ice water and stood at the sink sipping it and looking at my face in the mirror.

"You and Capablanca," I said.

It is one of Marlowe's typically self-reflecting conclusions. His striving is for order, predictability, understanding, for which chess master Capablanca serves as model; but he keeps discovering chaos, ambiguity, stupidity. He is capable of recognizing his own irrational romantic idealism, but continues to long for "the justice we dream of but don't find." He is the face on both sides of the mirror—one locked in a world of violence and evil, one free to wander the illusory world of nobler possibilities.

# 3

---

# A Sense of Foreboding:
## *The Lady in the Lake*
## *The Little Sister*

"Nobody ever knows what anybody else will do, sister. A cop knows that much."

*The Lady in the Lake*

In its simplest form, *The Lady in the Lake* (1943) tells the story of a vain, greedy, jealous woman who kills three people in a misguided attempt to free herself of personal entanglements. She is then herself killed by her former husband, who meets his own ignominious death at the hands of a young soldier. Significantly, World War II, a major distraction for Chandler (and the world) at the time, is here insinuated into his fiction. The story is sustained by one of the oldest tricks in the genre, mistaken identity, but the cleverness with which it is managed leaves the reader aghast at his own willingness to be duped. Perhaps the most engaging thing about the book is that Chandler is able to maintain this illusion, and even to mock what he is doing, without the reader being the wiser until the very end.

Yet the "trickiness" of the plot should not distract us from the tone behind it. Chandler's biographer, Frank MacShane, has called attention to the fact that this is "a somber book because it concentrates on those who are caught up in the system of Southern Cali-

fornia instead of those who direct it. . . . The novel is about all
the middlemen who are forced to conform to the style and habits
of a materialistic world."

The first such middleman Marlowe meets is Derace Kingsley,
a cosmetics company executive. Despite a flashy showroom and
office, he admits to Marlowe: "I have a good job here, but a job is
all it is. I can't stand scandal." The scandal he fears involves his
wife, who has been missing for a month. A telegram from her said
she was going to Mexico to divorce Kingsley and marry a local,
less-than-wealthy playboy, Chris Lavery. But her car has shown up
abandoned in a San Bernardino hotel garage, and Kingsley has
recently happened into Lavery who says he doesn't know anything
about the wife's plans.

The chance meeting between Kingsley and Lavery, which
draws Marlowe into the story, is only the first such coincidence of a
long series in the book. Coincidence, in fact, becomes a central
theme and allows Chandler both to comment on the role of chance
in the world and to parody the genre's frequent dependence on
monumental coincidences as plot resolvers. Chandler's plot is not
merely unraveled by chance; it plays upon chance as a shaper of
life.

Marlowe encounters the novel's second curious coincidence at
Little Fawn Lake, the spot from which Kingsley's wife Crystal disappeared. Another woman from the same area, Muriel Chess, apparently disappeared on the same day that Crystal did. Immediately,
our trained detective minds, and Marlowe's, perceive the possibility
of a confusion of identities. But that idea is short-lived; Muriel
Chess is momentarily shown to have been lying at the bottom of
the lake for the entire month. Despite the fact that Marlowe speaks
of the body as "the thing that had been a woman," we accept
its identification as Muriel for two very good reasons. First, it is
made by her husband, who initially suggests that she had a motive
for suicide, but who then recants and confesses to her murder. And
secondly, the telegram and car argue that Crystal was alive and
well after she left Little Fawn Lake.

The man who must deal with the problem most immediately
is Jim Patton—chief of police, fire chief, deputy sheriff, constable,
and chamber of commerce of Puma Point. Able to exist as an individual outside the bureaucracies of big-city police departments,

Patton is Chandler's most endearing lawman and the only source of comic relief in this otherwise gloomy book. Patton is a large, tobacco-chewing, lumbering man in a cowboy hat. For "eighty a month, cabin, firewood and electricity," he presides over his territory with a general benevolence. He is presently involved in a reelection campaign and carries in his car a sign which reads: "VOTERS, ATTENTION! KEEP JIM PATTON CONSTABLE. HE IS TOO OLD TO GO TO WORK." Marlowe "liked everything about him."

Though they remain adversaries to a degree, Marlowe and Patton become jointly involved in the case of Muriel Chess. As they do so, it appears likely that her husband, Bill, may in fact be responsible for her death, and they spend considerable time and energy trying to prove him either innocent or guilty.

The scene of their investigation, the California highlands, takes on a symbolic dimension. On more than one occasion, tame deer interfere with Marlowe's work. Their presence, as well as the lush, paradisical descriptions of the terrain, sends an echo of Eden through the story. By contrast, there are also the neon signs, shooting galleries, juke boxes, "and behind all this out on the lake the hard barking roar of the speedboats going nowhere at all and acting as though they were racing with death." Something is amiss in Eden. The cold reality of modern-day Bay City has begun to penetrate even the romantic purity of Puma Point.

One harbinger of this encroachment came in the form of a tough, big-city cop named DeSoto. Six weeks in the past, he visited Puma Point searching for a woman named Mildred Haviland. The photo he carried looked a lot like Muriel Chess, but he got no cooperation from the local people because he was just "a big roughneck with damn poor manners."

Marlowe finally meets this man DeSoto who is actually Lieutenant Degarmo of the Bay City police. His interest in the case involves yet another coincidence. It seems that a Dr. Almore of Bay City recently lost his wife under curious circumstances that were quickly hushed up. Dr. Almore's nurse at the time was Mildred Haviland, the woman DeSoto/Degarmo was looking for. Coincidentally, Crystal Kingsley was one of Almore's patients. And Chris Lavery, the man whom Crystal said she was marrying in Mexico, was the person who found Mrs. Almore's body. As Marlowe explains it to police Captain Webber, it was Mildred Haviland

who put Mrs. Almore to bed the night she was found dead in
the garage, and who, if there was any hanky-panky about that,
might know who it was, and be bribed or scared into leaving
town shortly thereafter. . . .

And at that point . . . you run into a real basic coincidence,
the only one I'm willing to admit in the whole picture. For this
Mildred Haviland met a man named Bill Chess in a Riverside
beer parlor and for reasons of her own married him and went to
live with him at Little Fawn Lake. And Little Fawn Lake was
the property of a man whose wife was intimate with Lavery,
who had found Mrs. Almore's body. That's what I call a real
coincidence. It can't be anything else but, but it's basic, fundamental. Everything else flows from it.

What flows from it, finally, is the truth—a truth quite serious
in its implications as social criticism but quite humorous as self-
parody of the detective genre. That truth comes to Marlowe when
he goes to convey money to Crystal Kingsley on behalf of her husband when she suddenly reappears needing cash to get out of town.
Marlowe reluctantly agrees to take it in order to get a chance to
talk to her. In the course of their conversation, he realizes that this
woman is not Crystal Kingsley at all; she is Muriel Chess/Mildred
Haviland. As this realization dawns, he continues to speak to her as
if she were Crystal and as if he were trying to get information
from her about Muriel in a conversation laden with irony. He says:

"Muriel Chess was really a girl called Mildred Haviland, who
had been Dr. Almore's office nurse."
"That's a queer coincidence," she said wonderingly. "I knew
Bill met her in Riverside. I didn't know how or under what
circumstance or where she came from. Dr. Almore's office, eh?
It doesn't have to mean anything, does it?"
I said, "No. I guess it's a genuine coincidence. They do hap-
pen."

As the scene progresses, she pulls a gun on Marlowe and his ironic,
mocking tone continues:

"I've never liked this scene," I said. "Detective confronts murderer. Murderer produces gun, points same at detective. Murderer tells detective the whole sad story, wasting a lot of val-

uable time, even if in the end murderer did shoot detective. Only murderer never does. Something always happens to prevent it. The gods don't like this scene either. They always manage to spoil it."

At this point, of course, the story is essentially over. Marlowe has deciphered the case and confronted the murderer. The only problem is that the murderer is holding a gun on him. But as Chandler writes for Marlowe this clipped summary of a hundred tired detective plots, we can almost see him gleefully admitting that he has written himself into a corner and preparing us for yet another parody of yet another standard resolver of plots—the *deus ex machina*. Without warning, without explanation, and as if from nowhere, a large figure of a man appears at Marlowe's periphery and knocks him out. The man, we learn later, had been hiding behind the curtain—still another tired old plotting device that has been around for centuries, since *Hamlet* at least.

Suddenly the story is no longer over. When Marlowe regains consciousness, Muriel/Mildred is dead beside him, circumstances have been arranged to make him look guilty, a heavy hand is pounding on the door, and there are still ten chapters left for him to clear himself and bring the real killer to justice.

The scene which does finally resolve the plot also brings it full circle. The villain from behind the curtain makes his final mistake by displaying an arrogant disregard for the wartime sentries posted at Puma Lake dam; he drives by them without stopping. As the young sergeant explains in very unimpassioned prose,

> "Guy didn't stop for the sentry. . . . Damn near knocked him off the road. The sentry in the middle of the bridge had to jump fast to get missed. The one at this end had enough. He called the guy to halt. Guy kept going. . . . Orders are to shoot in a case like that. . . . The sentry shot. . . . This is where he went off."

As the body is pulled from the car at the bottom of the canyon, Marlowe comments that it was "something that had been a man." The phrase echoes "the thing that had been a woman" line from earlier

and closes the novel with a macabre sense of justice. At least all the
murderers in the book have met their own deaths. But the device
also provides a neat structural balance for the plot and underlines
other interesting parallels developed in the story.

For example, early in the novel, Bill Chess comments about
his relationships with women, "Jesus, what a sap a guy can be."
That remark is balanced much later by Adrienne Fromsett's comment that "Women—even decent women—make such ghastly mistakes about men." The male-female balance of murderers, victims,
and interpersonal problems gives the book a symmetry which is
new for Chandler and which provides at least some evidence for
refuting the charges of sexism often leveled against him (see Chapter 6).

Of the other curious parallels in the story, one of the more
interesting ones concerns Patton's remarks about the "only [other]
honest to God murder I ever had up here." He tells the story of
old Dad Meacham, an old prospector found murdered in his bed,
"a kindling axe in the back of his head," in the midst of winter.
The case was never really resolved, but as Andy, Patton's associate,
says: "Course we know who done it. Guy Pope done it. Only Guy
was dead nine days of pneumonia before we found Dad Meacham."
The peculiar irony of the murderer being dead before his victim
is found deftly parallels and foreshadows the central story of this
plot in which, because of the mistaken identities, the person we
*assume* to be the murderer has been dead all along.

Such mannered complications may well help explain why *The
Lady in the Lake* required four years to write. No doubt the conflicts and difficulties in Chandler's personal life, as well as the im-
pact of World War II, also contributed to its slow development.
The war, especially, concerned Chandler; it intrudes into the book's
opening paragraph where a sidewalk made of rubber blocks is
being torn up "to give to the government," and through the guards
on the dam, it is central to the story's resolution. But the development and control of this carefully balanced plot was surely the
major factor in its slow evolution from previously published short
stories to finished novel, an evolution examined in greater detail in
Chapter 5.

The book expands upon those stories to draw a portrait of

evil finding its way even into society's remotest, most idyllic hideaways. Evil has escaped the city and reveals itself as a product of individual avarice and passion capable of carrying on quite well outside the modern urban wilderness.

But, beyond its general thematic stance, the novel also offers us insight into Chandler's approach to his craft. Although he despised the demands placed on him by the genre for neatly dovetailed plots, the evidence of *The Lady in the Lake* suggests that he was here attempting to demonstrate both that he could write such a plot and that he could parody the very exercise simultaneously. The plot is a fairly simple one, complicated by the old trick of mistaken identity. But it is sustained and rendered unique by the things about which Chandler truly cared—the language itself and the distinctive tone and narrative style which is Philip Marlowe.

When *The Little Sister* appeared in 1949, it was attacked by Anthony Boucher in the *New York Times Book Review* for "its scathing hatred of the human race." Other critics have also berated its misanthropic aspects and Chandler himself asserted that "it's the only book of mine I have actively disliked. It was written in a bad mood and I think that comes through."

Indeed, there are aspects of the novel which suggest a genuine absence of human values; seven people meet their deaths here while blackmail, greed, and envy divide friendships and families alike. But there are also elements of the novel which mark Chandler's further development as a writer. Its plot resolution exhibits a more sophisticated ambiguity as Marlowe achieves new insight into his own inescapable connection with this debased society. And, as an emblem of degradation, the movie industry provides extensive material here for the first time in the novels.

The story opens with a "small, neat, rather prissy-looking girl with primly smooth brown hair and rimless glasses" calling on Marlowe for help in locating her missing brother. She has come from Manhattan, Kansas, and can only afford to pay him twenty dollars.

A tone of parody is established from the beginning, chiefly through literary allusions which echo through the story. The girl's name is Orfamay Quest, and Marlowe says about her, ominously, that "nobody ever looked less like Lady Macbeth." We recognize again Chandler's not-so-subtle burlesque of the chivalric romance, combined this time with a focus on lusts for power not unlike those which obsess the characters of Shakespeare's *Macbeth*.

What Orfamay doesn't tell Marlowe is that she has a half-sister who is a rising Hollywood starlet using the name Mavis Weld. Mavis rooms with a tall, dark bombshell named Delores Gonzales, and both of them have friends among the local mobster circuit. The plot is concerned primarily with the variety of people who are attempting to make a profit from Mavis's rising career and from the damage which their knowledge of her association with gangsters might do to that career.

The brother, Orrin Quest, for whom Orfamay is searching, appears to have been blackmailing his own sister, Mavis, with photographs he took of her with a mobster named Steelgrave. A couple of lesser gangsters have apparently learned of Orrin's scheme and tried to horn in. Delores Gonzales proves, finally, to be a major figure in a plan to play off these rival elements against each other for her own reward and without regard for friendship. And even little sister Orfamay appears in the end to have had no nobler motivation behind her trip to California than to insure that she and her domineering mother back in Kansas were getting their fair share of brother Orrin's "business."

The book portrays gangsters against gangsters, friends against friends, and family against family—all for the greater glory of the almighty dollar and the power associated with it. But what is at the core of this human disaster? At least a part of the answer is Hollywood.

While we may agree with Frank MacShane that *The Little Sister* is not "a real Hollywood novel," in the sense that it does not attempt a complete portrait of that phenomenon, clearly Chandler is concerned here with the effects of Hollywood and the Hollywood mentality on individuals and, by extension, on society. Marlowe's statement on the subject is powerful—and damning:

> Wonderful what Hollywood will do to a nobody. It will make a radiant glamour queen out of a drab little wench who ought to be ironing a truck driver's shirts, a he-man hero with shining eyes and brilliant smile reeking of sexual charm out of some overgrown kid who was meant to go to work with a lunch box.

Out of a Texas car hop with the literacy of a character in a comic strip it will make an international courtesan, married six times to six millionaires and so blasé and decadent at the end of it that her idea of a thrill is to seduce a furniture mover in a sweaty undershirt.

And by remote control it might even take a small town prig like Orrin Quest and make an ice-pick murderer out of him in a matter of months, elevating his simple meanness into the classic sadism of the multiple killer.

The book's analysis of Hollywood extends to the moguls at the top as well as these nobodies being absorbed from the bottom. At one point, the plot draws Marlowe onto a studio lot in an attempt to contact Mavis. In a small patio, he confronts an elegantly dressed, elderly gentleman who is occupied with three boxer dogs—watching them dig up some begonias and observing the hierarchical order of their urination. The man is Jules Oppenheimer, who runs the "financial end" of the studio. Among his rambling remarks, he points out that "The motion picture business is the only business in the world in which you can make all the mistakes there are and still make money." And, he adds, "Doesn't matter a damn what they [the moviemakers] do or how they do it. Just give me fifteen hundred theatres." Clearly both ends of the Hollywood spectrum are seen to operate from morally bankrupt, socially decadent postures; for everyone from baron to would-be starlet, all morality goes by the boards in the pursuit of fame and fortune.

But this bankruptcy and decadence is not strictly limited to Hollywood. Behind Orrin and Orfamay, back in Manhattan, Kansas, stands a pious and arrogant mother whose sense of her own self-importance is symbolized by her denial of tobacco to her stroke-afflicted husband because the church needs the money more than he needs such superfluities. Moreover, Mom appears to have prompted Orfamay's trip to California and her vicious manipulations of both her siblings which ultimately nets Orfamay one thousand dollars in cash at the expense of her brother's life.

It is not a pretty story. A large and powerful industry based on illusion transforms the youth from America's heartland into conniving, sadistic automatons, and the family, which we expect to resist such impulses, only aggravates this lust for power. The conflicting forces stirred up by this bizarre plot allow for no simple resolution. Indeed, the ending that Chandler finally did contrive marks a perceptible change in his handling of the mystery novel and in Marlowe's comprehension of his peculiar fictional world.

As he was finishing *The Little Sister,* Chandler wrote a friend, concerning that resolution: "In the end I was faced with a choice between a clear but boring explanation of who shot who, and more or less letting it hang in the air on the theory that who cared anyway, it wasn't and couldn't pretend to be a proper mystery." It is not "a proper mystery" in the sense that it refuses to establish simple cause-effect relationships and pin the guilt, finally, on a single character. This disregard for the genre's demand for straightforward puzzles is, of course, not new with *The Little Sister,* but this novel does leave a great deal more "hanging in the air" than any of its predecessors. And its ambiguity takes its toll on Marlowe. Near the end of the book, he muses: "Sometimes when I'm low I try to reason it out. But it gets too complicated. The whole damn case was that way."

The illusoriness of Hollywood and of human action seem to have converged. Marlowe has watched the whole drama unfold and still it makes no sense. Another of his musings draws the parallel between the real action of life and the ephemeral action of the theatre: "The play was over. I was sitting in the empty theatre. The curtain was down and projected on it dimly I could see the action. But already some of the actors were getting vague and unreal. The little sister above all. In a couple of days I would forget what she looked like."

Marlowe has finally gotten himself involved in a case which has no coherent explanation or, perhaps more accurately, which admits of far too many explanations. Consider Steelgrave's murder, for example. Mavis is found with the body and a warm gun and confesses to the murder. But later information suggests Orfamay may have been responsible; Delores supports that theory. But, in the final chapter, Marlowe appears convinced that Delores was herself responsible, though he is never explicit—aside from some circumstantial conjecturing—about why he thinks so. He does suggest, approvingly, that Mavis is the only one of the lot with guts to stand up for principles and that "last night she proved she was willing to destroy herself" in order to protect her little sister. But Delores undercuts his romantic rhapsodizing with the reminder "if

she was not acting," and we and Marlowe realize that we are
caught in a trap. In a world where illusion has become the coin of
the realm, we are not likely ever to uncover the truth about characters' motives. The old theme of the stark discrepancy between
appearance and reality lurks here too. And, in one chapter in particular, Chandler explores the theme in a manner unique in all his
writings.

In that chapter (Chapter 30), Marlowe is under arrest, await-
ing interrogation on the subject of Steelgrave's murder. A short,
thin man sits across a table from him dealing cards. Given the
gun in his shoulder holster, Marlowe assumes he is a cop, whose
job, he figures, must be to get a confession from him. But the man's
role is never clarified; he contends that his mission is only to "establish a mood." Conversation is cautious and oblique on both sides.
Much is made of the man's hands; he is, in fact, described in terms
of them:

> You could see he was a man who loved to move his hands, to
> make neat inconspicuous motions with them, motions without
> any special meaning, but smooth and flowing and light as swans-
> down. They gave him a feel of delicate things delicately done,
> but not weak.

The man is a pianist, as it turns out, and there is some talk of
Mozart. He also gives a brief demonstration of his magician-like
skills with a gun.

In the course of their cryptic conversation, there is finally mention of one plot-related item. The police, he says, are convinced
that Marlowe "never shot anybody. . . . We got you figured long
ago." Though he agrees with Marlowe that the cops may be glad
to have had Steelgrave shot, he explains, "they don't like the way
it was done." Throughout the scene, the dramatic intensity is undercut by Marlowe's asides of "perfect casting"—suggesting his skepti-
cism—and by both men's obvious awareness of the roles they are
playing and which are expected of them.

And at the end of the scene, we and Marlowe are left with the
eerie feeling that the whole thing may have been an apparition.
As Christy French, the officer in charge of the case, walks into
the room, Marlowe says:

I looked from him to the little man across the table. But he
wasn't there anymore. The cards weren't there either. Nothing
was there but a chair pushed in neatly to the table and the dishes
we had eaten off gathered on a tray. For a moment I had that
creepy feeling.

Far from resolving the mystery, the scene only increases the in-
trigue. It smacks of Chandler's notion of the "fantastic story" in
which ordinary characters find themselves in extraordinary, almost
Kafkaesque circumstances. Its absurdist stance is heightened by the
characters' insistence on communicating by talking around issues,
even by a direct attempt to avoid communication altogether. The
chapter is indeed mysterious, but it is also a good example of the
compulsion Chandler felt to expand the dimensions of the detective
story.

Another chapter in this book also stands out as atypical. In
Chapter 13, Marlowe is just beginning to assimilate the early facts
in the case and has just left Mavis and Delores after their first
meeting. His mood is at once cynical and introspective. He wanders
into tirades against the decadence of California and the movie mentality, but consistently he brings himself up short with the thought,
"Hold it, Marlowe, you're not human tonight." Even while railing
against the fast food "feed 'em and throw 'em out" establishments
and the people who stand in line to eat at them, he admits that
he himself has stopped to eat at such places and adds, "They're
just restless. Like you. They have to get the car out and go some-
where. Sucker-bait for the racketeers that have taken over the
restaurants. Here we go again. You're not human tonight, Marlowe."

Ultimately, his thoughts turn to the case and he wonders:

Who am I cutting my throat for this time? A blonde with sexy
eyes and too many door keys? A girl from Manhattan, Kansas?
I don't know. All I know is that something isn't what it seems
and the old tired but always reliable hunch tells me that if
the hand is played the way it is dealt the wrong person is going
to lose the pot. Is that my business? Well, what is my business?
Do I know? Did I ever know? Let's not go into that. You're not
human tonight, Marlowe. Maybe I never was nor ever will be.
Maybe I'm an ectoplasm with a private license. Maybe we all

get like this in the cold half-lit world where always the wrong
thing happens and never the right.

Marlowe is forced here to recognize his own connection with the
restlessness on which this exploitative society feeds. As the chapter
ends, his restlessness draws him, curiously, to a movie, where his
admission price will only further the system which provides such
stereotypes as women who are "always going up a long curving
staircase to change their clothes" and men who are "always taking
monogrammed cigarettes out of expensive cases and snapping expensive lighters at each other." The irony of his own involvement
in this self-perpetuating cycle is not lost on Marlowe. This is the
most explicit statement so far of his recognition of the pervasive
human weaknesses which have spawned the illusions of California
and of his own entanglement with those weaknesses.

His reaction is to try to live up to his own personal code of
justice which knows "that something isn't what it seems" and which
strives to keep "the wrong person" from "losing the pot." If he ac-
complishes anything hopeful in the book, it is to save Mavis Weld's
career from being ruined by all the plotting against her. But the
nature of the movie business described in *The Little Sister* makes
even that accomplishment ring hollow. Marlowe must recognize that
there is little he can do about our seemingly inevitable slide toward
unreality. The outlook is decidedly pessimistic. But beyond its black
foreboding, *The Little Sister* is also a considerably better work of
fiction than is generally credited. In its complications of family,
organized crime, and Hollywood, it achieves a panorama of the
modern condition which is new for Chandler. And in its discovery
of ways to demonstrate Marlowe's connection with the human weaknesses on which the story turns, it provides new insight into his
central character. It is a fitting prelude to Chandler's next and, in
many ways, most ambitious novel, *The Long Goodbye.*

# 4

## The Last Struggles:
### *The Long Goodbye*
### *Playback*

"It isn't money I want. It's some sort of understanding of what the hell I'm doing and why."
*Playback*

*The Long Goodbye* (1954) is Chandler's most personal novel and
his most ambitious. It is at once his most autobiographical work
and his boldest attempt to exceed the confines of the detective
mystery. Natasha Spender, Chandler's friend and confidante in his
last years, has called attention to the three obvious self-portraits
which populate the book. Young Terry Lennox is an emotionally and
physically scarred war hero with an English accent and English
manners who wanders rather aimlessly about under the influence
of an overblown sense of the dramatic. Roger Wade is an aging,
embittered, drunken writer of popular fiction given to self-loathing
and writer's *angst*. And then there is Marlowe. In Spender's biographical interpretation, he is the ideal self, "the conscience which
punished the Roger Wade within him though not without commen-
dation for achievement . . . and befriended the Terry Lennox within,
not without censure." Although this tripartite self-examination is
indeed a primary source of the book's fascination, it is hardly the
only one.

The organization of this novel is of considerable interest as

well since Chandler here succeeds in expanding the story well beyond its central mystery plot. His selection of characters, locales,
and situations gives him abundant opportunity for digressions on a
wide variety of topics—and the asides frequently grow into small
essays. Roger Wade, the writer, delivers several of these sermon-
ettes on such diverse subjects as Freud, drunks, prayer, money,
homosexuals, and the writer's dependence on similes. Harlan Potter,
a wealthy entrepreneur, discourses ironically on Man, democracy,
newspapers and consumerism. Inclusion of the publisher's agent,
Howard Spencer, provides a forum for discussing the publishing
business in general and historical romances in particular. And Marlowe himself delivers a number of these brief essays on subjects ranging from jails, blonds, and public relations to nursing homes, lawyers,
and TV commercials. Chandler has been criticized for interrupting
his plot with these apparently extraneous, often splenetic interludes.
Such criticism, however, demonstrates rather traditional expectations
of detective mysteries and totally neglects the larger story which
Chandler has here set himself to tell.

On its most straightforward level, *The Long Goodbye* is a story
of friendship established and friendship betrayed. But on a grander
scale that story is only the microcosm of a more general social
deterioration. A letter to his agent which accompanied the first
draft of the story enlightens these larger concerns. In that letter,
Chandler bemoans the genre's preference for "constant action" over
character development and allows that he has become too "complicated and unsure" to satisfy that demand. His interests lay
instead in "moral dilemmas, rather than in who cracked who on
the head" and he continues:

> Anyhow I wrote this as I wanted to because I can do that now.
> I didn't care *whether the mystery was fairly obvious,* but I
> cared about the people, about this strange corrupt world we
> live in, and how any man who tried to be honest looks in the
> end either sentimental or plain foolish. (Italics are Chandler's.)

The asides, then, taken as sketches of basic elements of "this strange
corrupt world we live in" are essential to the elucidation of Chandler's larger, social concerns. Frequently, they demonstrate how the

world has resolved its "moral dilemmas"—most often in favor of corporate profit or personal greed. And, set against that broader background, the story of Terry Lennox provides a specific situation through which we, as readers, can experience the trauma of a reasonably conscious and sensitive man attempting to cope with this corrupt and alienating world.

Marlowe first spots Terry Lennox outside a club called The Dancers. (The same club figured prominently in *The Little Sister*.) Lennox is a very polite but uncoordinated drunk who is having trouble getting himself into a Rolls Royce. His female companion and the parking lot attendant have very little patience with him, and, when he finally slides out onto the pavement, Marlowe intervenes and is left holding him up as the Rolls glides off. In an offhand remark, Marlowe tellingly foreshadows the likely outcome of such random involvement in other people's lives: "I guess it's always a mistake to interfere with a drunk. Even if he knows and likes you he is always liable to haul off and poke you in the teeth." Such is the dilemma of Marlowe's knight-errantry; his code draws him to the magnanimous gesture despite the fact that his experience argues that such actions frequently result, at least figuratively, in a "poke in the teeth."

But Marlowe makes the effort nonetheless. After he gets Lennox sobered up, he doesn't see him again for some weeks. When he does, Lennox is stumbling drunk again—on the street this time —and again Marlowe comes to the rescue, barely saving him on this occasion from a trip to the drunk tank with a couple of cops who have been eyeing his behavior.

Around Christmas, Marlowe gets a hundred-dollar check from Lennox with his thanks and the news that he is now remarried to his wealthy wife Sylvia, daughter of multimillionaire Harlan Potter. But by March things are evidently falling apart again, and Lennox walks into Marlowe's office looking for conversation and a drinking companion.

Over the next couple of months, afternoon gimlets become something of a ritual between the two. Though Marlowe's manners keep him from delving too pointedly into the details of Terry Lennox's life, we do discover that he was reared in an orphanage in Salt Lake City and that, as he says, he considers himself a weak character, without guts or ambition. I caught the brass ring and it shocked me to find out it wasn't gold. A guy like me has one big moment in his life, one perfect swing on the high trapeze. Then he spends the rest of his time trying not to fall off the sidewalk into the gutter.

Lennox's disillusionment is the product of a shattering war experience and a marriage which has failed—not once, but twice—to live up to his very romantic, American dream. Though Marlowe is not totally unsympathetic, he finally becomes upset by Lennox's excessive self-absorption. As he says, "You talk too damn much . . . and it's too damn much about you." Though he feels badly about the scene only a few minutes later, Marlowe leaves Lennox sitting at the bar, walks out, and a month-long hiatus develops.

The next time Marlowe sees Lennox he is ringing his doorbell at five o'clock in the morning, carrying a gun, looking like he hasn't slept for a week, and demanding that Marlowe drive him to Tijuana to catch a plane. He claims to be in a lot of trouble, but Marlowe, recognizing himself to be caught in a dilemma between the law and a friend, cautions Lennox against telling him too much. Though Lennox can hardly help talking about his wife, Marlowe carefully steers the conversation to suggest that Lennox has found his wife dead drunk and with another man. We sense that Marlowe clearly understands that Lennox is telling him his wife is dead, but Marlowe is concerned about the delicacy of his own position with the police. At bottom, he is certain that he knows Lennox well enough to be sure that he wouldn't kill his wife—despite the fact that Lennox freely admits the murder just before he boards the plane. With cryptic exchanges like "I have reasons" from Lennox and "So have I" from Marlowe, the two make their goodbyes and we have been set up for the novel's preoccupation with causes.

This book is perpetually asking the question "Why?" Frequently the query involves Marlowe's own introspection: Why does he stick with being a private investigator? Why does he take certain actions and not others while he is on a case? The concern so pervades the novel that at one point it even provides the author an occasion for self-parody: an extended joke about California's weather and the smog ends, "Once in a while a whole day would be clear, nobody quite knew why." Though the remark calls our attention to the absurdity of pushing one's quest for causes too hard, it also recalls the cosmic mystery still evident in the play of sunlight in the bushes at the end of *The Big Sleep*. Concern for causes, of course, is a basic convention of the genre. But one of Chandler's recurrent themes is the practical, human limits of such concerns, and nowhere is he more explicit about that theme than in *The Long Goodbye*.

By the time Marlowe gets back from Tijuana, the police have already begun putting together their version of events. Marlowe's lack of cooperation with their investigation gets him taken downtown and very nearly beaten up, but a call from the commissioner puts an end to the questioning. Evidently some political conflict over disposition of the case has developed between the police and the district attorney's office, and Marlowe is the beneficiary of the delay caused by the wrangle. Nevertheless, he spends three days in jail until a lawyer appears mysteriously to offer assistance. But the attorney proves unnecessary. We and Marlowe soon learn that Terry Lennox has committed suicide in Otatoclan, Mexico, after writing out a full confession to the murder of his wife. As far as the police are concerned, "The Lennox case is closed, mister. There ain't any Lennox case." And Marlowe is released.

But when Marlowe gets back to his office, Sewell Endicott, the lawyer who visited him in jail, calls with further offers of help and the admonition, "Don't be too certain you're in the clear." And that incident is followed by an even more curious one. A flashily dressed, very self-satisfied man arrives at Marlowe's office, looks him over carefully, and pronounces: "Tarzan on a big red scooter." It is not at all clear what the line means, but the man is obviously pleased with it and with himself. He is Menendez, a local racketeer and, according to his own slangy characterization, "a big bad man, Marlowe. I make lots of dough. I got to make lots of dough to juice the guys I got to juice in order to make lots of dough to juice the guys I got to juice." Menendez speaks virtually a private language, and language, too, is Chandler's subject here. Menendez' argot forces both the reader and Marlowe into an interpretive role and results in an ambiguity which draws attention to the imprecise nature of language itself. Marlowe and Menendez do communicate, but more on a visceral than a cerebral level. And we are left to wonder about the meaning of "Tarzan on a big red scooter."

Menendez' principal concern is to convince Marlowe to forget

the Lennox case. His connection with Lennox stems from his having been in the same military unit with him and Randy Starr, another racketeer. As he explains, "We were three guys in a foxhole
eating." A delayed mortar shell fell right in their midst and Lennox,
instinctively, grabbed it and threw it out. But as he did so, the shell
exploded and severely injured one side of his face; Lennox still
bears a plastic surgery scar from the incident. As Lennox lay injured, "the krauts mount an attack and the next thing we know we
ain't there any more." Lennox was held prisoner for a year and a
half, and was located after the war through Menendez' and Starr's
efforts; "we made plenty in the black market. . . . We could afford
it." Menendez claims to be upset because Lennox went to Marlowe
when he was in trouble rather than to him and Starr, the men
who owed him their lives. Menendez doesn't want Marlowe "trying
to make . . . dough or publicity out of the Lennox case. . . . Terry's
dead and we don't want him bothered any more. The guy suffered
too much." Though the explanation begins to make some sort of
sense, Marlowe's reaction is typically contemptuous; "A hoodlum
with sentiment," he says. "That slays me." And Marlowe is left to
wonder about the curious coincidence of Menendez' warnings
coming so close on the heels of Sewell Endicott's.

Three days pass, and a ring of the office telephone launches
the plot into what appears, at first, to be a totally unrelated case.
The man on the phone is Howard Spencer, representative of a
New York publishing house, and he is seeking Marlowe's services
on a delicate matter that he wishes to discuss the following morning. At home that evening, Marlowe discovers a letter from Terry
Lennox. The letter guesses that Marlowe has already figured out
that the brutality of the murder meant that Terry didn't do it—"So
something is very sour. But it doesn't matter, not in the least. The
main thing now is to save an unnecessary and useless scandal. Her
father and her sister never did me any harm." The letter goes on
to mock the disparity between fiction and reality:

> I have written a confession. I feel a little sick and more than a
> little scared. You read about these situations in books, but you
> don't read the truth. When it happens to you, when all you
> have left is the gun in your pocket, when you are cornered
> in a dirty little hotel in a strange country, and have only one

way out—believe me, pal, there is nothing elevating or dramatic about it. It is just plain nasty and sordid and gray and grim.

The letter also includes a five-thousand dollar bill as "an apology for making you so much trouble and a token of esteem for a pretty decent guy." The letter gives Marlowe a sleepless night, but he does manage to make his 11 A.M. appointment with Howard Spencer.

Spencer's delicate problem concerns one Roger Wade, successful author of a number of best-selling historical romances. The problem is that Wade is given to "wild fits of drinking and temper" and is prone to disappearances when imbibing. Wade's wife, Eileen, is worried that someone may be blackmailing him, that "something from his past may have caught up with him." Spencer takes the more cynical view that Wade is just "a very talented guy who has been jarred loose from his self-control. He has made too much money writing junk for halfwits." We can already see here the numerous parallels drawn between Wade and Chandler's own biography: the drinking bouts, the disappearances, and the relative contempt for the genre which made him wealthy and famous. Such self-reflexive parallels manifest Chandler's considerable insight into his own idiosyncracies. And Marlowe's search for Wade, following one of his disappearances, provides other opportunities for Chandler to speak out on matters related to his own life. The search leads Marlowe to the environs of numerous physicians of questionable reputation and occasions several of his diatribes against doctors and medical institutions. Chandler, of course, especially in his last years, was frequently a patient in hospitals and rest homes. His own experiences are as surely at the root of this criticism of the medical profession as his own sensibilities and uncertainties are behind Wade's remarks on the writing profession: "I'm a writer," he says. "I'm supposed to understand what makes people tick. I don't understand one damn thing about anybody." Regardless of what Wade (or Chandler) does or does not understand, Marlowe gets him safely home and assumes his job is finished.

But a coincidental meeting a few days later begins to tie the stories of Roger Wade and Terry Lennox together. On a slow afternoon, Marlowe pulls Terry's last letter from his safe for another look and realizes that he never returned to Victor's, their favorite watering hole, for the memorial gimlet which the letter requested.

It strikes him as a fine afternoon for such an occasion, and, as he
is on his way, he reflects briefly on his feelings about Lennox:

> I thought of him with a vague sadness and with a puckering
> bitterness too. When I got to Victor's I almost kept going. Al-
> most, but not quite. I had too much of his money. He had made
> a fool of me but he had paid well for the privilege.

He stops in for the ritual gimlet; a woman in the bar is also
drinking gimlets and the coincidence draws them into conversation. Conversation proves the coincidence to run much deeper than
their taste in drinks. The woman is Linda Loring; she is the sister
of Terry Lennox's dead wife, Sylvia, and she is acquainted with
the Wades. The Lorings and the Wades all live in Idle Valley, a
name transparent in its social comment. (For a time, Chandler
considered calling this novel *Summer in Idle Valley*.)

Shortly, the Wades throw a party and Marlowe has an opportunity to become more familiar with this Idle Valley society. The
party disintegrates rather quickly into a round of accusations on
the order of who's-been-sleeping-with-whom, and Marlowe finds
himself on the terrace wondering "what the hell I was doing there."
The most significant plot information revealed here involves a story
told by Eileen Wade, Roger's wife, about her first husband. He was
a young man killed in the war whom she loved with "the wild,
mysterious, improbable kind of love that never comes but once."
Ironically, he had the same initials as Marlowe, but she never
speaks his name. She does, however, wear a unique military pendant on occasion, evidently in his memory.

The next few weeks find Marlowe, at the request of Howard
Spencer, periodically playing the role of babysitter for Roger Wade
as he tries to stay off the bottle long enough to do his writing. After
one particularly disconcerting session between the two, Marlowe
walks down to the lake shore to watch the speedboats and to con-
template his own entanglement in the lives of the Wades, the Lorings, and the Lennoxes.

When he walks back to the house, the door chimes are ringing.
Eileen has evidently locked herself out of the house, though the
circumstances appear fairly unusual. And when they next look in

on Wade, he is dead, the victim of a gunshot wound to the head. Suicide is a possibility, but the circumstances are also right for homicide. The houseboy, Candy, might have been implicated, but he was away at the time. Eileen is clearly suspected, but what motive would she have for killing him like this when she must have had so many other opportunities? She goes so far as to suggest that Marlowe did it, but he manages to remove himself from suspicion.

Shortly, Marlowe's own suspicions begin to take shape. His investigations concentrate on verifying Terry Lennox's past—his war record and his association with Menendez. One acquaintance who met Lennox in California says he knew him in New York as Paul Marston. The initials P.M., of course, are those of Eileen Wade's first husband, a man presumed to have been a casualty in the war. The key to this portion of the plot is the little military pendant Eileen wears. Marlowe does some research on the matter, discovers some inconsistencies in her account of the facts, confronts her with his evidence, and finally begins to deduce the truth.

Eileen, in fact, wed Paul Marston/Terry Lennox in England during the war, while he was on leave from his commando unit. He then disappeared, and was presumed taken prisoner, in the action which Menendez described. As she points out, "In October 1942, . . . Hitler issued an order that all Commando prisoners were to be turned over to the Gestapo. I think we all know what that meant. Torture and a nameless death in some Gestapo dungeon."

Understandably, when no news was forthcoming, she began to construct a new life for herself, and her marriage to Roger Wade was a central part of that life. But, in a chance meeting one afternoon at the Lorings', she discovered that the assumption on which she had ordered her life for years was mistaken. Marston/Lennox was there—and he was married to Linda's sister Sylvia, a woman whom Eileen describes as "that redheaded whore." "We were lost to each other," she says. "Why? . . . Oh, you wouldn't understand. What we had was lost. It could never be recovered." The romantic dream had been shattered—by world events, by time, and by the attendant changes in the personal lives of the two people who once lived that dream, if briefly. To make matters worse, Eileen is already aware of her husband Roger's continuing affair with Sylvia.

Like most of the other novels, this story is rooted in a conflict

between two women. In this case, one of the women has taken
from the other both the men about whom she has deeply cared.
Frustrated by the cosmic injustice of her romantic ideal disappear-
ing in a brutal, senseless war and then returning when it is "too
late" Eileen resorts to violence and murder.

But if Eileen is the murderer, how are we to explain Terry
Lennox's behavior? Our story is obviously not yet over. Marlowe's
continued probing of the case finally results in a visit from "a well-
dressed Mexican or Suramericano of some sort" who introduces himself as Cisco Maioranos. His mission is clearly to pacify Marlowe
with enough information about Lennox's death to bring a halt to
his investigation. But Marlowe catches him in inconsistencies, too,
and sets out to construct his own story.

Marlowe is of the opinion that Lennox's death in Mexico was
all a great hoax and that the hoax included an elaborate scheme
for persuading Sewell Endicott, the lawyer, of his death in order
to support his confession and to halt the investigation by the police.
And finally Marlowe recognizes Senor Maioranos as Terry Lennox
himself, Terry Lennox altered by further cosmetic surgery and nerve
grafts.

Lennox's story is:

> Look, I couldn't very well help what I did. . . . I didn't want
> anyone to get hurt. I wouldn't have had a dog's chance up here.
> A man can't figure every angle that quick. I was scared and I
> ran. What should I have done?

But Marlowe is uneasy with such glib explanations. He returns the
five-thousand dollar bill and says:

> I'm not sore at you. You're just that kind of guy. For a long
> time I couldn't figure you at all. You had nice ways and nice
> qualities, but there was something wrong. You had standards
> and you lived up to them, but they were personal. They had
> no relation to any kind of ethics or scruples. You were a nice
> guy because you had a nice nature. But you were just as happy
> with mugs or hoodlums as with honest men. Provided the hood-
> lums spoke fairly good English and had fairly acceptable table
> manners. You're a moral defeatist. I think maybe the war did
> it and again I think maybe you were born that way.

And in the end, Marlowe is left sitting at his desk, listening to Lennox's footsteps echo down the hall, and wondering *why*. Given his previous behavior, we may expect that he will shortly find appropriate circumstances for drinking himself into a moderate stupor.

By way of sorting out this rather complex story, it may be instructive at this point to consider the motives of the principal characters. Eileen Wade kills Sylvia Lennox for reasons about which we can only conjecture. Her explanations of the event are obviously false, as Marlowe leads her to admit, and her suicide prevents any closer scrutiny of her actions. We may assume that she killed Sylvia Lennox in a passionate rage brought on by the loss of two husbands to the same unprincipled woman; and she finally killed Roger Wade because he was becoming too emotionally unstable to insure her secret. Ample evidence suggests that their relationship had been long on the rocks anyway; a result, no doubt, of Eileen's lingering, romantic commitment to her first love, lost to the horrors of war. Whatever the precise workings of her mind, we can easily sympathize with her loss and then with her abject frustration when this lost husband returns mysteriously, married to a woman who is having an affair with her present husband. And always, in the background, there is the war, that grand madness beyond her control without which her story would have had a decidedly different ending.

Roger Wade's state of mind can best be explained in terms of his recognition of his own contribution to Eileen's hysteria, his attempt to cover for Eileen, his own loss of both Sylvia and Eileen, and his attempt to maintain himself afloat financially with a writing career which has developed along disconcertingly simplistic lines. Under the competing pressures of his writer's drive to explain, to make sense of the world, and his very human impulse to hide his own guilt and protect those for whom he cares, he finally verges on madness and is destroyed.

But Terry Lennox is the real focus of the book. Marlowe's final assessment of him is that he has only private standards, with no sense of a general ethic. Lennox himself admits to living his life as an act, that "an act is all there is," but, as with Eileen, our judgment of him is mitigated by our recognition of the horrifying past which he has survived. Even Marlowe will not judge him because he recognizes the limits of his own ability to comprehend another man's pain, a pain articulated by Lennox only in the vague phrases, "I got badly hurt and it wasn't any fun with those Nazi doctors. It did something to me."

In the midst of all this, of course, is Phillip Marlowe who describes himself only as "a romantic. . . . I hear voices crying in the night and I go see what's the matter." But the line is delivered with some ironic reflection, and, by the end of the novel, we and Marlowe have sufficient reason to question the practicality of such an approach to a fallen world. The world, in fact, shows ample signs of having changed in such a way as to make romantic heroes obsolete. War on a new scale has shattered at least one man's sense of any ethic beyond the personal, and Lennox's experiences and the coincidences surrounding them plant the seeds of destruction in several other lives. Chandler has clearly accomplished his announced purpose of making Marlowe look "in the end either sentimental or plain foolish" for trying to be an honest man in the face of "this strange corrupt world we live in."

The strangeness and corruption of the modern world are most evident in the lives of two other central characters, Harlan Potter and Mendy Menendez. Potter is another man with a very private sense of principle and with the economic power to enforce it. *Control*, in a world apparently out of control, is his forte. As Marlowe explains his encounter with Potter to Linda Loring,

> He explained civilization to me. . . . He's going to let it go on for a little while longer. But it better be careful and not interfere with his private life. If it does, he's apt to make a phone call to God and cancel the order.

Mendy Menendez is yet another man operating from a very private ethic, but, despite his gangsterism, his motives here are the apparently noble ones of aiding a friend or, perhaps more accurately, repaying a debt. Either way, as Lennox points out, "You're not the only guy in the world that has no price tag, Marlowe." And we must also recognize with Lennox that Mendy "has a heart," though we may respond with Marlowe, "So has a snake."

In this confused, amoral world, perhaps we can come closest to understanding Marlowe's predicament by recalling Menendez' characterization of him as "Tarzan on a big red scooter." Our first reaction to the statement is to wonder who this man is and what, if anything, his remark means. As the story progresses, we realize that there is sense to be made of the statement; it is not totally meaningless. Tarzan, of course, is a character out of the heroic mold, but "Tarzan on a big red scooter" suggests the hero well out of his element, in a new age, and the more ludicrous for being on "a big red scooter" rather than in one of the limousines which Menendez and the Idle Valley crowd have made essential. Marlowe, like Tarzan, is drawn to the grand, heroic act but the modern world has rendered such acts "plain foolish."

*The Long Goodbye* is clearly Chandler's last great effort to push the mystery novel out of its stereotyped niche. Unlike any of its predecessors, it takes on the whole modern society as its subject. It concentrates its examination of the effects of that society on three specific individuals: Terry Lennox is a casualty of the mass insanity of modern war; Roger Wade is a product of the great entertainment (read: escape) industry and the modern perversion of art; Marlowe is the spirit of another age striving desperately to maintain a sense of decency. And all three, of course, are projections of different aspects of the character of Raymond Chandler. The book turns both outward toward the world and inward toward the self. It recognizes human weakness. It ends on a puzzled note of quiet reflection. And it does so with the conviction that the world's problems are finally the problems of individual human beings. Terry Lennox may well have the war and a tyrannical father-in-law to blame for much of his plight, but he surrenders rather easily when he discovers that "the brass ring . . . wasn't gold." Roger Wade may well blame his hysterical wife and a modern longing for artistic pabulum for his unhappy career, but he must also recognize his own contributions to both. And Marlowe is himself left to wonder what it is he wants, exactly, and what it is that he expects of other people. He is unsure, finally, and his uncertainty underscores the book's ambiguity. Either the world is dominated by forces truly beyond individual control or individuals have merely acquiesced to those unprincipled elements of a society whose only measures of value are power and money. Neither alternative is pleasant. The plight of the individual in the modern world is the essence of Marlowe's dilemma at the end of *The Long Goodbye;* we are uncertain of what we want and, by extension, of who we are.

*Playback* (1958) has been called "undistinguished," "a forgettable work," and "a sad hoked-up job." While it lacks much of the plot and character complication which mark the earlier books, it still displays the characteristic Chandlerian wit and provides certain insights into the author and his attitude toward his work in his later years.

In truth, the plot is the slightest of all the books. Marlowe is hired to follow a young woman who is evidently running from something which happened in her past. Ultimately, she is shown to be guiltless, at least in the legal sense, in the matter from which she is fleeing. But, in the course of her travels, she encounters a blackmailer and, through him, becomes involved in a rather vague struggle for power within the mob. Finally, her tormentor, the cause of her flight, appears on the scene, is unmasked as an arrogant man with no real case against her, and all is more or less well.

Unusual aspects of the book include Marlowe's increased sexual interest in the two primary female characters, a genuinely sympathetic treatment of big-city police, inclusion of some quite lengthy scenes which have little or nothing to do with the plot line, and, rather astonishingly for a Chandler novel, an apparent disinterest in the final fate of characters: the two principle female characters each simply "disappear" from the story without a real resolution.

Betty Mayfield, the central figure in the novel, is last seen on her way back to her hotel talking of her possible love for Clark Brandon, the ex-racketeer from Kansas City who has apparently taken over the Esmeralda rackets. In Marlowe's last verbal exchange with Betty, he says:

> "Could you really love a man like that?"
> "A woman loves a man. Not what he is. And he may not have meant it."
> "Goodbye, Betty. I gave it what I had, but it wasn't enough."

For Marlowe, Betty's action represents a personal failure; his best "wasn't enough." Her overly simple romanticism threatens to seduce her into endless relationships with Brandon and similar reprehensible types—despite Marlowe's efforts to help her, and despite her own recent experience with the dark side of human nature.

Marlowe's relationship with Helen Vermilyea also ends in a kind of failure, and romantic failure, in fact, is a central theme of the book. Miss Vermilyea is secretary to Clyde Umney, the lawyer who hires Marlowe to tail Betty Mayfield. Marlowe's relationship with Helen begins as strictly business; she handles all the technical arrangements relating to his pay and expenses. Her manner is at once tough and flirtatious. Their verbal battles provide the book with much of what life it has through the early chapters until Marlowe one day asks, "What are you doing tonight? And don't tell me you're going out with four sailors again." Her response is, "I've got friends who could cut you down so small you'd need a stepladder to put your shoes on." To which Marlowe replies, appreciatively, "Somebody did a lot of hard work on that one. . . . But hard work's no substitute for talent." They burst into laughter and she later offers, "You're kind of cute in a low-down sort of way."

Behind that repartee, which establishes the relationship between the two, lies a comment on the writer's recognition of his own diminishing powers. When Chandler advised other writers about how to convey the Marlowe character for radio shows or movies, one of his central tenets was that Marlowe should not always be given the punch line. Here Miss Vermilyea has the punch line and the exchange highlights an important dimension of the work as a whole. *Playback*, like Miss Vermilyea's retort, bears the mark of a writer struggling to equal former achievements; it is obviously the product of age and hard work rather than of the facility of youthful talent. But it is also the creation of a mind quite aware of its shortcomings relative to its former greatness; it is a work of determination. In that, it is interesting to recall Chandler's own comments on the late novel of another man he greatly admired, Hemingway's *Across the River and into the Trees*. While he recognized its relatively low merits, he also appreciated it as the struggle of a great writer. He rebuked the "primping second-guessers who call themselves critics" by pointing out that the book demonstrated "the difference between a champ and a knife thrower. The champ may have lost his stuff temporarily or permanently, he can't be sure. But when he can no longer throw his hard high one, he throws his heart instead. He throws something. He just doesn't walk off the mound and weep."

Part of Chandler's striving was to deal somewhat more realistically with male–female struggles than previous books had allowed him. Toward that end, Marlowe and Helen Vermilyea establish a rendezvous for the evening and the two finally wind up in bed together. Each, however, is restrained from a genuine commitment by memories of past loves. Marlowe does not want to make love to her in his own apartment because "I had a dream here once, a year and a half ago. There's still a shred of it left. I'd like it to stay in charge." Helen's memory is of her former husband, a jet pilot killed in a plane crash. Her confused notions of romance are graphically articulated in this brief statement following their coital encounter:

> "I hate you," she said with her mouth against mine. "Not for this, but because perfection never comes twice and with us it came too soon. And I'll never see you again and I don't want to. It would have to be forever or not at all."

With that, she calls him a taxi and we, and Marlowe, never see her again. Such statements and actions manifest an extreme idea of love as one pure encounter never to be equalled, always invoking an impossible standard from the past—an idea which has difficulty coexisting with the vagaries and ambiguities of day-to-day existence.

Marlowe himself suffers from a similar problem which finds its clearest expression in the book's final chapter. Characteristically, he has returned home from a case despondent over his relative ineffectiveness in the face of a world which refuses to conform to his stylized notions of decorum. He goes so far as to deny himself a drink, saying "Alcohol was no cure for this. Nothing was any cure but the hard inner heart that asked for nothing from anyone." His instinct counsels withdrawal and a hardening of the spirit against the cold, insensitive world.

But, shortly, that attitude undergoes a radical transformation. The telephone rings and Linda Loring, Marlowe's dream from a year and a half ago (in *The Long Goodbye*), is on the other end. She is calling from Paris and asking Marlowe to marry her. After a brief lover's argument over who is to pay for whose plane ticket —Marlowe insists on paying—Marlowe is a changed man. His romantic reverie ends: "The air was full of music."

In *The Poodle Springs Story*, the novel he was working on at his death, Chandler has Marlowe married to Linda Loring. The inevitable conflicts growing out of their totally different economic and social backgrounds were to provide a major subplot for the book. In the fragment of the story which survives, Marlowe is looking for office space in Poodle Springs (a parody of Palm Springs) and discovers that he is preceded everywhere by gossip about his wife's wealth. Chandler intended their relationship to be "a running fight interspersed with amorous interludes," but in *Playback*, Linda's appearance serves a considerably more harmonious function.

Her phone call in the last chapter, which has no connection at all to the plot line, is virtually a *deus ex machina* resolution which culminates a long series of reflections on the past, or playbacks, that structure the novel. Helen Vermilyea's brief affair with Marlowe recalls her stake in the past too clearly and brings their relationship to an end. Betty Mayfield has crossed the country to flee her involvement with a man who died of a broken neck only to encounter another man dead from similar causes. Clark Brandon is obviously re-creating in Esmeralda his racketeering past in Kansas City. And Linda Loring surfaces from Marlowe's past to rescue him, at least momentarily, from the depths of depression and to underscore the role of fate and chance in a world not nearly so ordered as Marlowe's dated sensibilities might desire.

The uncertainties of life that these playbacks recollect are articulated most clearly by Henry Clarendon IV, a character whose autobiographical echoes are likewise evident. Clarendon, for example, is described as "old, all right, but a long way from feeble and a long way from dim." Chandler, of course, was approaching seventy as he was finishing this novel. Clarendon also wears gloves and never shakes hands; Chandler wore gloves in his last years to protect his hands which suffered from arthritis and skin maladies, and he considered shaking hands an overdone American custom.

Through Clarendon, Chandler allows himself a direct voice in the narrative and the opportunity to comment on various issues— not all of which are directly related to the plot. Clarendon comments irreverently on subjects ranging from military intelligence to

God. He points out that "Military Intelligence is an expression which contains an interior fallacy." He speaks of the medical profession in terms of "starched white dragons. . . . that awful loveless hospital food. . . . and . . . the silent horror of the doctor's smile." In a passage which blends comments about God and art, he suggests that

> if God were omnipotent and omniscient in any literal sense, he wouldn't have bothered to make the universe at all. There is no success where there is no possibility of failure, no art without the resistance of the medium. Is it blasphemy to suggest that God has his bad days when nothing goes right, and that God's days are very, very long?

The remarks draw close parallels between the creative processes of God and those of the writer/artist. Each, according to Clarendon, is driven toward success by the very possibility of failure; each creates out of the very resistance to creation. Chandler, certainly, had his own bad days when nothing went right, his own "very, very long" days. Is it not obvious here that Chandler is chronicling his own struggle with the resistance of the medium and the likely "possibility of failure?" Certainly, Clarendon is Chandler's spokesman when he comments:

> How strange it is that man's finest aspirations, dirty little animal that he is, his finest actions also, his great and unselfish heroism, his constant daily courage in a harsh world—how strange that these things should be so much finer than his fate on this earth. That has to be somehow made reasonable. Don't tell me that honor is merely a chemical reaction or that a man who deliberately gives his life for another is merely following a behavior pattern.

The drive to render the struggle for heroism "reasonable" in the face of certain death in a harsh world can be seen as the central impulse behind both Chandler as author and Marlowe as detective. The resulting tension created by this irresolvable problem (noble actions vs. a meaningless end) defines both Chandler's real-life despondency and the despondency which his private detective experiences at the end of nearly every book. The struggle, whether Chandler's or Marlowe's, is to maintain an ethic, a code, which is rapidly slipping into the shadows of the past. The fear is of an impending chaos. The overpowering drive is to render it all "reasonable." But, as the end of *Playback* suggests, even Marlowe—despite his experience—can still be directed by a phone call in the night, the irrational promise of romance, and delirious thoughts of hope and a mystical salvation. Chandler is no more complex or incomprehensible than his age, and *Playback* is no less than the last pitch from the heart of an articulate witness of a dying order and a dawning confusion.

# 5

## The Raw Material:
## The Short Stories

"All at once, it was too logical."
*"Red Wind"*

Chandler's novels, of course, followed his noteworthy career as a writer of short stories for popular "pulp" magazines. A survey of those stories gives evidence of considerable experimentation in subject matter, style, point of view, and detective types which contributed to the novels' later success. Some of the stories were "cannibalized," as Chandler put it, into the novels, and a close look at that process allows us the unusual opportunity of observing the writer at work, transforming his own earlier, simpler material into the broader vision of the later books. But even the stories that weren't cannibalized have much to teach us about Chandler's development as a writer, and it seems appropriate here to look back at those stories for the deeper appreciation they may give us of the novels and the novelist.

From a purely artistic perspective some of these twenty-two detective/mystery short stories are considerably more successful than others. All, we should bear in mind, were written for a very specific market with rather rigorous demands for violence. Some meet that demand in a fairly standard manner; others manage considerable innovation within that framework. That innovation, of

course, and the alterations which occurred between the stories
and the novels, are our primary interests.

*The Big Sleep, Farewell, My Lovely,* and *The Lady in the
Lake* are the novels which owe most of their plots to the stories.
*The Big Sleep* evolved primarily from "Killer in the Rain" and "The
Curtain," with minor borrowing from "The Man Who Liked Dogs."
*Farewell, My Lovely* combines elements from "Try the Girl" and
"Mandarin's Jade." And *The Lady in the Lake* draws largely on "Bay
City Blues" and "The Lady in the Lake" while borrowing a few
details from "No Crime in the Mountains." The other four novels
are, with minor exceptions, completely original creations.

Initially, Chandler's system of "cannibalization" worked well.
*The Big Sleep,* for example, was completed in only three months.
But *The Lady in the Lake* required over four years to produce. The
slow pace at which it was developed can be attributed partly to
disturbances in the world and within Chandler's own life; the war,
for example, was a powerful distraction. But, it also seems likely
that technical problems encountered in combining the stories for
this novel may have contributed to that slow development and persuaded Chandler, finally, to abandon the cannibalizing technique.
A comparison of the novel with its source stories highlights the
difficulties.

The short story "The Lady in the Lake" (January 1939) tells
only that part of the novel's story that occurs at Little Fawn Lake.
It is a much simpler tale and the motives which direct it are decidedly different from those of the novel. The detective in the
short story, John Dalmas, is hired by a man named Howard Melton (cf. Derace Kingsley in the novel) to find his wife who has
disappeared from their lake cabin. At the cabin, Dalmas meets
Bill Haines (cf. Bill Cross) and, shortly, a body presumed to be
Haines's wife Beryl is discovered in the lake. Dalmas has already
discovered the dead body of Lance Goodwin (cf. Chris Lavery)
with whom Mrs. Melton was supposed to have disappeared. Clev-
erly, Dalmas tricks Melton and the female killer into appearing at
Goodwin's at the same time. The woman is Beryl Haines—who
has evidently been in league with Melton all along to help him
get rid of his wife and claim her wealth. Melton hired Dalmas
because he needed the body positively identified to legitimize the
inheritance. The mechanics of this plot obviously resemble that

part of the novel involving the body in the lake and the resulting confusion of identities. The characters also have recognizable analogues in the novel. But it is, finally, a rather simple story of a stock type: a man has attempted to rid himself of his wife and cover the deed with a case of mistaken identity.

"Bay City Blues" (June 1938) is the source of the other half of *The Lady in the Lake*. It is a story of dope, jealousy, and murder surrounding a Dr. Austrian (cf. Almore), "a guy that runs around all night keeping movie hams from having pink elephants for breakfast." Dr. Austrian's wife is found dead, presumably of carbon monoxide poisoning, much as Mrs. Almore is in the novel. The person who is evidently responsible for her death is Helen Matson, Dr. Austrian's nurse (cf. Mildred Haviland). But the doctor covers for his nurse, evidently because of his romantic involvement with her, and the police, who are obviously being paid off, cover for the doctor. That cover-up falls apart, though, because of the combined monetary and frustrated romantic interests of two other men closely associated with Helen, and because of the competition for control between the local political and racketeering circles. When Helen Matson is herself murdered later and the detective, Johnny Dalmas, is framed for it, the story begins to make sense to him. He is left, as he mockingly describes himself, "a miracle man. . . . the great American detective—unpaid" to explain the tale all "from a pinch of dust, just like the Vienna police."

Part of the "pinch of dust" that allows him to unravel the case concerns two identical pairs of green velvet slippers, which also appear in the novel. But another factor in the resolution involves Dalmas' inferences from a scene of viciousness unlike anything in the novels. A tough cop named DeSpain (cf. Degarmo) beats up a politico-rackets figure called Big Chin in a protracted display of sadism that weaves in and out of the narrative for seven pages. The very theatrical nature of this brutality finally persuades Dalmas that DeSpain is the real killer trying to cover his own guilt with another man's forced confession. By making this cruelty and violence serve as an essential clue in the plot's resolution, Chandler does manage—barely—to avoid the charge that such scenes are totally gratuitous. But the savagery was also, he recognized, a virtually mandatory ingredient of stories intended for the "pulp" market. Another example of Chandler's acquiescence to such demands, also from "Bay City Blues," is Dalmas' description of Harry Matson, the victim of another beating, just before his death: "One of his temples was a pulp, . . . The one straining finger that wasn't white had been pounded to shreds as far as the second joint. Sharp splinters of bone stuck out of the mangled flesh. Something that might once have been a fingernail looked now like a ragged splinter of glass." Such grotesque scenes are most common in the early short stories, become less frequent in the later ones, and are generally avoided in the novels.

But Chandler's transformation of these two stories into a novel involve considerably more than rendering the violence less explicitly. "The Lady in the Lake," though it uses the mistaken identity ploy on which the novel so heavily depends, is essentially a straightforward story of misguided love and murder for profit. "Bay City Blues," with its inclusion of decadent dope doctors preying on the artificial wealth of Hollywood, along with the story's confusion of love, political, and racketeering interests, comes closer to the complexity of the novel but still lacks much of the novel's intricacy and mystery.

The basic device which Chandler employed to combine these stories was, of course, entangling the lives of the central female characters from each story. (The importance of a conflict between two women as a structural device in other novels is further discussed in Chapter 8.) Though much of the plotting of the novel is evident in the stories, this collision of the lives of two women from different parts of California's corrupt society allows Chandler to develop the larger theme of coincidence and the fate of bit players in a villainous and alien world. The novel is also able to expand its scope to include the real war in progress at the time, using it not only as background and commentary but also, finally, to bring the tale to its just and provocative end. A character consumed by his own petty lusts for power meets his death because of his refusal to comprehend the larger struggle of which his own is only a minuscule reflection.

Frank MacShane has argued that Chandler's "experience with the pulps was an essential stage in his development as a novelist, for it taught him to mistrust the mind of the short story writer, which, he later acknowledged, 'gets by on an idea or a character or a twist without any real dramatic development.'" The creation of *The Lady in the Lake* lends credence to that argument. The short story "The Lady in the Lake" gets by on the mistaken identity twist; "Bay City Blues" gets by on the almost satanic character of Lieutenant DeSpain. Such techniques are simply not sufficient to sustain the longer work. Though the novel relies on the stories for basic plot lines, it, like all of Chandler's novels, is concerned with plot only to the extent that plot functions as a frame for his "dramatic development" of character and motivation and for his experiments in style. Character, motivation, and style, we must never forget, were his central interests.

Chandler's stylistic experiments and his keen awareness of language are particularly evident in a comparison of specific scenes which occur in both the short stories and the novels. *The Big Sleep* offers many such opportunities for comparison. To begin with one very brief example, Marlowe says of Vivian Sternwood at their last meeting in the novel, "She was in oyster-white lounging pajamas trimmed with white fur, cut as flowingly as a summer sea frothing on the beach of some small and exclusive island." In "The Curtain," the sentence reads, "She was in an oyster-white something, with white fur at the cuffs and collar and around the bottom." To say that she is dressed in an "oyster-white something" may, in fact, suggest this woman's essential nebulousness, but to specify "oyster-white lounging pajamas" and to include the idyllic "frothing sea" simile renders both her appearance and her state of mind with far greater precision. The casually romantic flair of her dress and carriage bespeak a desire to divorce herself from the harsh, imperfect world in which she is trapped. Her clothes suggest a certain escapism in the face of cruel facts. From just this tiny bit of elaboration we garner a sense of the warring elements at work in this woman's psyche. It is the kind of descriptive detail which the detective short story, with its demand for constant action, does not readily allow.

The scene of Marlowe's first meeting with Vivian demonstrates similar differences between Chandler the writer of short stories and Chandler the novelist. In "The Curtain," we read:

> This room had a white carpet from wall to wall. Ivory drapes of immense height lay tumbled casually on the white carpet inside the many windows. The windows stared towards the dark

foothills, and the air beyond the glass was dark too. It hadn't
started to rain yet, but there was a feeling of pressure in the
atmosphere.

In *The Big Sleep*, the paragraph has been expanded:

This room was too big, the ceiling was too high, the doors were
too tall, and the white carpet that went from wall to wall looked
like a fresh fall of snow at Lake Arrowhead. There were full-
length mirrors and crystal doodads all over the place. The ivory
furniture had chromium on it, and the enormous ivory drapes
lay tumbled on the white carpet a yard from the windows. The
white made the ivory look dirty and the ivory made the white
look bled out. The windows stared towards the darkening foothills. It was going to rain soon. There was pressure in the air
already.

The first paragraph only describes the stark contrast between
the white interior and the darkness outside. The second, while re-
taining that essential contrast, expands to comment on the paradoxical core of the Sternwood family: the material excess that is
incapable of disguising their moral vacuity. Even their decorative
attempt at purity looks phony and bled out by the contrasts in
white. And no amount of decoration can deny the gathering darkness on the other side of the windows. This "bled out" image is
echoed near the very end of the novel when Vivian says: "I knew
Eddie Mars would bleed me white, but I didn't care. I had to have
help and I could only get it from somebody like him." The General
has already supplied a context for interpreting that remark when
he told Marlowe early on that neither of his children "has any more
moral sense than a cat. Neither have I. No Sternwood ever had."
In such a world, devoid of the moral sense, being "bled white" in exchange for "help" is only what one expects. And though we may,
in fact, develop a certain sympathy for Vivian and her plight, the
literal description of her colorless life implies a figurative colorlessness which, we begin to understand, dooms her to an unceasing
commerce with Eddie Mars or men like him. The contrast between
the two paragraphs demonstrates both the flexibility of the novel
format in comparison with the strict limits of the pulp short story
and also Chandler's knack for exploiting that flexibility.

The greater restrictions of the short story were responsible, especially in his early stories, for limiting Chandler's subject matter as well as his style. His first story, "Blackmailers Don't Shoot" (December 1933), explores a theme common to many of Chandler's early efforts. Its fury arises from the internal struggles of rival racketeers and its social comment from the close connection between the rackets and the "authorities"—police, lawyers, and politicians. "Blackmailers Don't Shoot" is, in fact, one of Chandler's better early stories. It complicates the organized crime story with a young movie starlet, Rhonda Farr, who, in her attempt to adapt to the wickedness of the town and profession in which she finds herself, contrives a public relations stunt which backfires. The initial captivation of the story derives from the rather curious circumstance that the detective, Mallory, appears to be one of the blackmailers. But Mallory's act proves to be only part of a game which he is playing for his employer, a minor rackets figure named Landrey. The object of the game is, evidently, to revive the lost romance between Landrey and Rhonda Farr, the starlet. Finally, as is typical of Chandler even in this very first story, the facts of the matter are decidedly unclear. We are left with the police explanations, which are self-satisfying and internally consistent, but which we, and Mallory, know to be false.

In its obscuring of the truth, indeed in its suggestion that the truth is hopelessly elusive, the story establishes a pattern evident throughout the Chandler canon. Mallory here, as Marlowe frequently does in the novels, constructs several alternative possibilities for why things happened the way they did. None of them are totally satisfying. And yet we sense in this story motivations basic to human nature and not overly complex. Mallory speaks of Landrey's motives in these simple, if oblique, lines: "He crossed everybody up and then he crossed himself. He played too many parts and got his lines mixed. He was gun-drunk. When he got a rod in his hand he had to shoot somebody. Somebody shot back." It is a tale of cunning, self-deception, and a random violence directed only at "somebody" in a mysterious world where that "somebody" can shoot back.

The story is decidedly Chandlerian—in its refusal to offer a simple resolution, in its choice of subject matter and suggestion of a general corruption, and in its flashes of descriptive power and brilliant dialogue. But, given the stylistic excellence which the novels have led us to expect, there are also lapses here which startle the ear. Two such shortcomings occur on the story's first page. In the opening description of Mallory, we read: "His hair was crisp and black, ever so faintly touched with grey, as by an almost diffident hand." The word *diffident* calls undue attention to itself as rather exaggerated for the context. And our first look at the starlet begins: "Rhonda Farr was very beautiful." It is the kind of flat abstraction which we do not expect of Chandler and which rarely recurs after this first effort.

His next two stories, "Smart-Aleck Kill" (July 1934) and "Finger Man" (October 1934), are very similar to "Blackmailers Don't Shoot" in their subject. Both chronicle a series of struggles within the rackets organizations and highlight the involvement of an important political figure in those organizations. But because they lack some of the complications of "Blackmailers"—the confused and confusing starlet, the bizarre love interest as catalyst—these are rather slight stories by comparison.

But Chandler's fourth story, "Killer in the Rain" (January 1935), marks a new direction in which organized crime is no longer the central motif. The first story to be "cannibalized" (for *The Big Sleep*), it concerns Carmen and the smut-lending business of a man named Steiner (cf. Geiger). The story ends with a shootout at Joe Marty's apartment which is similar to, but more violent than, the scene at Joe Brody's in the novel. But, though the story shares many features of the novel, its most curious twist is in the handling of the father. Carmen's father here is a "former Pittsburgh steelworker, truck guard, all-round muscle stiff" who wandered to California and blundered into a fortune when oil was discovered on his property. A curious touch is added to the story when he confesses, "Carmen—she's not my kid at all. I just picked her up in Smoky, a little baby in the street. She didn't have nobody. I guess maybe I steal her, huh?" And the strange quality of the tale is compounded when he asserts further that he is now in love with her and wants to marry her. His concern is that she has developed an interest in this Steiner character, and he wants help in ending it.

Though there is still an element of organized crime lurking in the shadows, the story focuses on this bizarre romance which leaves the detective, in anticipation of Marlowe, wondering "why I had taken the trouble" and feeling "tired and old and not much use to anybody." Curiously, the detective is never given a name in this story; he is just an anonymous first-person narrator.

Throughout his career as a short-story writer, Chandler was obviously searching for the ideal detective and the ideal narrative stance. His next story, "Nevada Gas" (June 1935), attempts to bridge the gap between first- and third-person narration. It opens with a powerful scene of vindictiveness which a first-person detective narrator could not describe—simply because he could not have been on the scene. But once the detective, Johnny DeRuse, enters the story, he is followed very closely—in the manner of a first-person narration. Chandler was here striving to fuse the objectivity of the third-person point of view with the subjectivity of the first person. The dichotomy was one which he toyed with throughout his early career. First-person narration, of course, limits an author to the perceptions and experiences of his narrator. Third-person narration, on the other hand, denies the author the immediacy of his detective's sensibilities and reactions. The objectivity of the third person obviously appealed to Chandler early; six of his first nine stories are written from that point of view. But then a string of first-person stories reversed that pattern, and eleven of his last thirteen detective stories have first-person narrators. Chandler's final resolution of this subjective-objective problem in the novels, of course, was to create a first-person narrator, Marlowe, with a very objective narrative style. His very "objectivity," then, provides a veil for what are obviously very intense subjective responses to the events of the novels, and Chandler is able to achieve some of the virtues of both points of view.

Much as objectivity, or the illusion of objectivity, is one of Chandler's focal interests, also paramount is his concern for truth and illusions which pass for truth. His next story, "Spanish Blood" (November 1935), addresses that issue. Superficially, it seems yet another rackets and political corruption story, but, by its conclusion, we have reason to question such assumptions. A unique feature of the story is that its investigator is a policeman, Detective Lieutenant Sam Delaguerra. The end of the story reveals two clear —and clearly different—explanations for the murder, the one we and Sam know to be true and the one the police hierarchy believes. For his own reasons, Sam lets the "official" version stand, and we, as readers, are left with one of Chandler's most explicit statements on the subject of illusion and the sinister reality only barely beneath its surface.

"Guns at Cyrano's" (January 1936) also plays upon the now standard mobsters and corrupt politicians theme, but it offers a new twist in the introduction of Ted Carmady, a detective who reappears in several subsequent stories. Carmady describes himself "grimly" as "the All-American sucker. . . . A guy that plays with the help and carries the torch for stray broads." He is a man who "used to be a private dick" but who has avoided the profession of late. Unlike Marlowe, he doesn't need the money. As he explains to Jean Adrian, his girlfriend in the story, he has rather an ambivalent attitude toward the "dirty money" he lives on:

> My dad made it out of crooked sewerage and paving contracts, out of gambling concessions, appointment pay-offs, even vice, I daresay. He made it every rotten way there is to make money in city politics. And when it was made and there was nothing left to do but sit and look at it, he died and left it to me. It hasn't brought me any fun either. I always hope it's going to, but it never does. Because I'm his pup, his blood, reared in the same gutter. I'm worse than a tramp, angel. I'm a guy that lives on crooked dough and doesn't even do his own stealing.

Carmady is thus set apart from Chandler's typical characters by the guilt at the root of his motives, a guilt which will not allow him to continue in his father's greedy footsteps. He is also set apart by the relationship he develops with Jean Adrian, herself less than noble, which finally promises at least the possibility of their future happiness together. In its holding out even the chance of an optimistic, romantic future, this is indeed a rare story for Chandler.

Chandler's other short-story detectives continue to display idiosyncracies in social position and professional background. Walter Gage, for example, also has money and a beautiful girlfriend; Pete Anglich is an undercover narcotics agent who also "used to be" a private investigator. But these rather superficial differences between them and the later Philip Marlowe are less striking than their similarities. All exhibit some degree of alienation; all are committed to high ideals against great odds; and, as the stories progress, they increasingly manifest more of the wisecracking wit that so distinguishes Marlowe in the novels. Though the detective is not called Marlowe until *The Big Sleep*, it is obvious, as Chandler himself said, that "he certainly had his genesis in two or three of the novelettes." Some of the short-story detectives are so like Marlowe, in fact, that their names were changed to Marlowe in reprinted editions without doing much damage to his character except making him appear more violent. But these were not Chandler's changes. Rather, he attributed them to "a base commerical motive" on the part of publishers.

This violent streak of the stories is particularly evident in the next one, "The Man Who Liked Dogs" (March 1936). But the style in which the violence is handled has a far greater ambition than simply to shock or to titillate. Consider this scene:

> The machine gun began to tear the door apart as I bawled into the ear of a bored desk sergeant.
> Pieces of plaster and wood flew like fists at an Irish wedding. Slugs jerked the body of Dr. Sundstrand as though a chill was shaking him back to life. I threw the phone away from me and grabbed Diana's guns and started in on the door for our side. Through a wide crack I could see cloth. I shot at that.

The description is highly visual and objective. Verbs, with support from a few aptly-placed similes, drive the action long. Adjectives and adverbs are rare. The terror of the scene is balanced by the simplicity of its telling, and the net effect is of a world of mayhem and madness passing for normalcy.

The story ends with a similar scene in which the narrator, Ted Carmady, tells us:

> The gun in my hand felt large and hot. I shot the dog, hating to do it. The dog rolled off Fulwider and I saw where a stray bullet had drilled the chief's forehead between the eyes, with the delicate exactness of pure chance.

The tale itself has a kind of "delicate exactness" not unlike the stray bullet squarely between the chief's eyes. But this is not an "exactness of pure chance"; rather, it is the studied exactness of a man absorbed by the mysteries and ironies of language. And Chandler's extraordinary power in using a simple language and a simple form to suggest the mysterious depths of human activity is the chief source of his narrative richness.

"Pickup on Noon Street" (May 1936) resembles Chandler's first story, "Blackmailers Don't Shoot." It is another tale of an ill-conceived, Hollywood publicity stunt which backfires and embroils the principal characters in yet another rackets power struggle. Its chief distinction lies in its further experimentation with street slang. The story opens with a man and woman walking past the Surprise Hotel. After the man's rather forceful attempt to pick her up, the woman replies: "Listen, you cheap grifter! . . . Keep your paws down, see! Tinhorns are dust to me. Dangle!" Such dialogue manifests Chandler's attentive ear and anticipates some of the speech patterns of the novels. But, beyond this, the story shows little innovation.

Chandler's next story, "Goldfish" (June 1936), takes several new tacks. For one thing, it forsakes the Southern California setting for a trip to Olympia, Washington, and, finally, to Westport, the westernmost point in the U.S. For another, it is a story of a crime from the past and the power of gossip, ultimately, to uncover it. Wally Sype spent fifteen years in Leavenworth for theft of the famous Leander pearls. The pearls were never recovered. But Wally made the mistake of talking about the job to his cellmate once; when the cellmate got out, he talked; and the string of talk finally leads to the literal end of the West where Sype, now in hiding, worries out his old age playing with goldfish. They're "like people," he says, "They get things wrong with them. . . . Some you can cure . . . and some you can't."

Both the comparison of the fish with people and the setting of this story at the limits of the West serve to give this tale a symbolic value which is new for Chandler. By the end of the tale, we have reason to wonder that if the fish are "like people," may it not be in their confined existence and their subjugation to powers outside their own tiny frame of influence? As the stories and novels develop, this theme of fate, coincidence, and a general helplessness in the face of imponderable forces will take on greater significance.

Elements of Chandler's next story, "The Curtain" (September 1936), have already been discussed in relation to the novel, *The Big Sleep*, which grew from it. The plot of the story has much in common with the novel, but, as usual, it is the differences which are most intriguing. The story opens, in fact, with a scene closely parallel to the opening of *The Long Goodbye* where Marlowe meets Terry Lennox. But the focus quickly shifts to an open concern for the whereabouts of Dud O'Mara (cf. Rusty Regan), a story always in the background in *The Big Sleep*. The figure in this story who later became Carmen in the novel is a child, Dade Winslow Trevillyan, son of the character who later becomes Vivian. The impetus of his actions is pure hatred, and precisely because of such simply characterized motivations, the story fails to maintain our interests. Though rather pedestrian in itself, this story, combined with "Killer in the Rain," constitutes the humble origins of one of Chandler's better novels.

His next two stories, "Try the Girl" (January 1937) and "Mandarin's Jade" (November 1937), were "cannibalized" to create *Farewell, My Lovely*. The two stories offer striking contrasts in their resolutions. "Try the Girl" is essentially the story of Steve Skalla's (cf. Moose Malloy) search for Beulah (cf. Velma). In the end, a central question is: Who killed Dave Marineau? Both Steve and Beulah seem intent on taking the blame. Beulah claims to have killed him because "he roughed me up and tried to blackmail me into something and I went and got the gun." But she bears no bruises or torn clothes to verify her version of the events. To simplify matters for the police, the detective (Ted Carmady again) roughs her up, waits for the bruises to set and darken, then takes her downtown where the police, because of her appearance, "didn't even think of holding her or checking her up." The ending is one of expediency rather than strict justice and, again, what the world is willing to accept as "truth" is, in fact, something less than that.

"Mandarin's Jade," on the other hand, contrives its ending considerably more neatly than does *Farewell, My Lovely*, which incorporated much of its story line. Here we have the story of the jade necklace being ransomed, but in this case, there is a much closer and more apparent relationship between Lindley Paul (cf. Lindsay Marriott) and Soukesian the Psychic (cf. Amthor). Soukesian is the brains and Paul is the finger for a high-class jewel ring—a relationship which is suggested in the novel but which is never proven and which remains obscured in the haze of possible causes for the book's actions. Here, the explanation of the crime is simplified; in the novel, precise causes remain mysterious.

This plot transformation, though, is only one aspect of the interest of "Mandarin's Jade." We also witness here a *style* in transition from the blood-and-gore, purely action-oriented early stories to the more pensive manner of the novels. For instance, when John Dalmas sits looking at Soukesian's card, he tells us:

> I had a rough idea what his racket would be and what kind of people would be his customers. And the bigger he was the less he would advertise. If you gave him enough time and paid him enough, he would cure anything from a tired husband to a grasshopper plague. He would be an expert in frustrated women, in tricky, tangled love affairs, in wandering boys who hadn't written home, in whether to sell the property now or hold it another year, in whether this part will hurt my type with my public or improve it. Even men would go to him—guys who bellowed like bulls around their own offices and were all cold mush inside just the same. But most of all, women—women with money, women with jewels, women who could be twisted like silk thread around a lean Asiatic finger.

The passage exhibits the brooding, almost cynical detective stance characteristic of the novels—he already has "a rough idea what his racket would be"; he's seen all this before. And it also demonstrates Chandler's attempt to find a way to get beyond the genre's demand for mayhem, to find a forum for commenting on the state of the world. Here, Dalmas makes the comment for him. He analyzes the society's problems as a general weakness of both men and women —an inability to deal intelligently with love and money, and a susceptibility to the illusions of people like Soukesian. It is the kind of passage on which the novels thrive, but which, in the short stories, runs the risk of appearing simply as excess baggage.

"Red Wind" (January 1938), in its dialogue, its tone, its descriptions, and its provocative implications, is another story that has many stylistic affinities with the novels. Its opening paragraph is one of Chandler's best:

> There was a desert wind blowing that night. It was one of those hot dry Santa Anas that come down through the mountain passes and curl your hair and make your nerves jump and your skin itch. On nights like that every booze party ends in a fight. Meek

little wives feel the edge of the carving knife and study their husbands' necks. Anything can happen. You can even get a full glass of beer at a cocktail lounge.

The wind establishes an atmosphere of general foreboding. The empathy which that wind evokes in people suggests their general frailty and the irrationality just beneath the illusion of order. The last line then undercuts the weightiness of the mood just created and makes it palatable. Such quizzical humor is characteristic of Marlowe in the novels and helps relieve his brooding cynicism. It is his humor which allows him to broach serious subjects obliquely.

In keeping with the ominous atmosphere established by the wind, the story involves some great and grave coincidences and is another which suspects the world of being well out of control. Its language asserts the point. After the cop has been told the story of the tale's first shooting three times, he says: "This dame interests me. And the killer called the guy Waldo, yet didn't seem to be anyways sure he would be in. I mean, if Waldo wasn't sure the dame would be here, nobody could be sure Waldo would be here." The narrator can only respond: "That's pretty deep." The language proves too imprecise to penetrate the essence of matters, a general failing that is, of course, another motif which emerges more forcefully in the longer works.

The story also exhibits the mocking tone characteristic of the novels. At one point, when we think the story is beginning to resolve itself, the central female character brings up the subject of her pearls. The narrator is taken aback:

> I might have jumped a little. It seemed as if there had been enough without pearls. . . .
> "All right," I said, "Tell me about the pearls. We have had a murder and a mystery woman and a mad killer and a heroic rescue and a police detective framed into making a false report. Now we will have pearls. All right—feed it to me."

The paragraph recapitulates all the standard plotting devices on which this and so many other mysteries depend. It calls attention to its own formula, ridicules it, but then accepts it and proceeds. In so doing, it also forces the reader to recognize the author's own self-consciousness about the stylized simplicity of his tale.

The story's finale also anticipates the endings of the novels. Although the pearls finally prove to be an essential element of the plot, they are not real. The real ones were evidently sold by one of the story's crooks who then substituted imitation ones. The detective (called Marlowe in most of the reprints of the story) has imitations made of the imitations and returns this second-generation set of fakes to their owner. The first set of fakes he takes with him to the beach. There he sits tossing the pearls one by one into the water, watching the splashes and the seagulls, contemplating the vegetation burned by the hot wind and the ocean that "looked cool and languid and just the same as ever," and thinking of Stan Phillips, the man who first purchased the original pearls and made a gift of them to Lola, setting the plot in motion. It is an ending with a definite Marlovian touch; the stories are beginning to find their meaning in the effect they have on the detective. His musing synthesizes all the appearance vs. reality motifs which have arisen in the story: the pearls have now been twice bastardized; the newspaper accounts of the action of the story aren't even close to the truth; and a police lieutenant has been framed by his own enthusiasm into taking credit for an arrest he didn't make and which later recoils against him.

The narrator accepts it all as quite believable. But he also needs the time alone with the "cool and languid and . . . same as ever" ocean to restore his sense of equilibrium. And it is in the contrast of his ability to cope and his obvious sense of loss and futility that the stories make their emotional impression on the reader. We feel, with the man tossing fake pearls into the ocean, the profound absurdity of the modern world, but we also sense with him the necessity and the possibility of carrying on. It is an experience not unlike catharsis.

"The King in Yellow" (March 1938) may seem less typical of Chandler because it avoids centering on the sentiments of the detective in the manner of "Red Wind" and so many other of Chandler's better stories. Rather, it examines a relationship between two brothers and a sister, the brothers being out to revenge their sister's death. Eventually, one brother tires of killing and the ever-widening circle of death which the first death set off and he puts an end to it, paradoxically, by killing his brother and committing suicide. But the story simply ends. Its third-person narration—one of Chandler's last uses of the third person—is incapable of the kind of emotive power which his first person narrators can convey. It is a flat ending to a comparatively slight story.

Chandler's next two stories, "Bay City Blues" (June 1938) and "The Lady in the Lake" (January 1939), have already been discussed as the sources for *The Lady in the Lake*. The story which followed them, "Pearls Are a Nuisance" (April 1939), is a fine example of Chandler's linguistic experimentation within the detective form and one of his better treatises on male camaraderie, a subject which was later to form the basis for *The Long Goodbye*. Walter Gage, the detective here, is a man with money, a beautiful girl-friend, and a formal diction which allows Chandler to achieve new heights of humor. He says things to people like, "Have the kindness to unlock the door," "I cast no aspersions . . . , I now suggest we repair to my apartment," and "The sunset hour is nigh. . . . and the morning glories furl themselves in sleep." Such language offers a dramatic contrast with the street slang of Henry Eichelberger, who is given to remarks like, "Bugs completely is what the guy is," or "Here's some mug finds out Lady Penruddock has a string of oyster fruit worth oodles of kale, and he does hisself a neat little box job and trots down to the fence."

"Pearls Are a Nuisance" is one of Chandler's funniest stories, and its humor is largely a result of this startling juxtaposition of languages. Moreover, these languages express two very diverse personalities whose interaction is the center of the comedy. Gage is a man of wealth and aristocratic pretensions; Eichelberger is a big, brutish chauffeur. Gage initially suspects Eichelberger of the pearl theft, but, in a series of brawls and heroic drinking bouts, the two become fast friends. Their friendship, in fact, is finally responsible for making the culprit "too soft to go through with the deal," and the story ends with what in comparison to the other stories is almost a general rejoicing. It argues well that Chandler had his lighter moments when he was truly able to divorce himself from the world's malaise and allow his sense of language play and the comedy of human relationships to have full rein.

His next story, "Trouble Is My Business" (August 1939), is another competent but slight story which plays upon the standard themes of blackmail, greed, and murder. Curiously, the villain here is another chauffeur who, this time, has a Dartmouth education. But the story displays little innovation. It is typical of the genre and evidence that Chandler could also, occasionally, be content with tried and true formulas.

But "I'll Be Waiting" (October 1939), which followed, is a curious piece of experimentation that mimics the romantic exploit of a knight in shining armor rescuing a tower-bound lady in distress. The knight in shining armor in this case is a "short, pale, paunchy, middle-aged man" named Tony Reseck who is the house dick at the Windermere Hotel. The lady in distress is a red-haired, violet-eyed, has-been nightclub singer named Eve Cressy who has "a tower room" in the hotel and who hasn't been outdoors in the five days since her arrival. Around her, but just outside her field of awareness, a rackets war is developing among the males of her world. Her ex-husband, Johnny Ralls, whom her testimony helped convict of manslaughter, is back in town. And his mob friends are after him for money which he presumably beat them out of. One of the mobsters suggests that Eve be moved from the hotel. But the detective Reseck has a sentimental attachment to her. He arranges, instead, to play the mobsters off against each other, getting people killed in the process. But Eve never knows what happened. And the last we see of her, she is asleep, curled up motionless, listening to the radio in a room off the lobby which is a private, little, mock-Edenic haven for this curious pair of platonic lovers. On one level, the story is a mock romance. But on another, the story argues that such sentimentality is a powerful shaper of life—even among these people who hardly fit the romantic stereotypes. That we are all, at bottom, motivated to some extent by such sentiments is one of Chandler's central tenets.

"No Crime in the Mountains" (September 1941) switches to a more topical theme. It is, in a sense, a war story. A German and a Japanese have set up a counterfeiting and smuggling operation at Puma Point in order to finance an Axis intelligence operation. John Evans, the detective, almost gets tipped off about it, but his informer is killed before they can talk. Evans is thus left to figure it out for himself and to stumble onto a number of other strange happenings in the process. He gets a lot of help from the local constable, a man named Barron, who is virtually a carbon copy of Tinchfield in "The Lady in the Lake" and Jim Patton, a central figure in the novel version of that story. But aside from Barron's countrified humor and the plot's wartime concerns, this too is a fairly standard story.

Eighteen years separate the publication of "No Crime in the Mountains" and that of Chandler's last detective short story, "The Pencil" (April 1959). In a brief introductory note to it, he explained that he had

> persistently refused to write short stories, because I think books are my natural element, but was persuaded to do this because people for whom I have a high regard seemed to want me to do it, and I have always wanted to write a story about the technique of the Syndicate's murders.

Marlowe is the detective here. His client is "a slightly fat man with a dishonest smile" named Ikky Rosenstein. He claims to be on the run from the mob because he's been penciled. As Marlowe later explains the term, "You have a list. You draw a line through a name with a pencil. The guy is as good as dead. The Outfit has reasons. . . . It's bookkeeping to them." As he also later explains, "I neither believed him nor disbelieved him. I took him on. There was no reason not to." The voice is decidedly Marlowe's—calm, detached, seen-it-all, a surface placidity masking a deeper trepidation—and it is Marlowe's voice that gives the story what distinction it has. It is a voice still capable of hilarious self-mockery, as we see when Marlowe tells us at one point:

> I bought a paperback and read it. I set my alarm watch for 6:30. The paperback scared me so badly that I put two guns under my pillow. . . . Then I asked myself why I was reading this drivel when I could have been memorizing *The Brothers Karamasov*.

But it is also a tired voice, telling a tired story, almost a cliché, as if filling out a form, walking the familiar tightrope between burlesque and sentimentalism and falling, finally, in the direction of the latter.

One of the story's most curious sentimental lapses concerns its resurrection of Anne Riordan, the wonderfully competent, too-good-to-be-true character from *Farewell, My Lovely*. In one conversation between them, she becomes perturbed by Marlowe's distant attitude and asks, straightforwardly, "How come I'm still a virgin at twenty-eight?" Marlowe's response is: "We need a few like you. . . . I've thought of you, I've wanted you, but that sweet clear look in your eyes tells me to lay off. . . . I've had too many women to deserve one like you." And as he walks out, he is thinking, "The women you get and the women you don't get—they live in different worlds. I don't sneer at either world. I live in both myself." The exchange is perplexing and finally unsatisfying. Marlowe is here defeated by his own romantic idealism. He is trapped within his own code. Anne is "too good" for him, he is "too shop-soiled" for her, and the story retreats from complication into stereotypes.

As a group, the stories display for us the mind of a technician in the midst of honing his craft. The crisp declarative style, plain descriptions, terse characterizations, sardonic wit, and ominous mood can all be seen here in their formative stages. But it is only in the novels that all those elements so characteristic of Chandler achieve their maturity. The difference is partly a matter of space —space to allow for dramatic and character development and to get away from the requisite, slavish devotion to plot. And it is partly a matter of the creation of the voice of Marlowe who, though he may appear in the stories in prototype, is only realized completely in the longer works. The novels, unlike the short stories, consistently make their impression upon the reader through the sympathy they evoke for this endearing, nobly motivated detective, and it is to him and his personality that we should next turn our attention.

# 6

# A Hero Out of Time:
# Philip Marlowe

> "Nobody understands me, Mrs. Loring. I'm enig-
> matic."
>
> *The Long Goodbye*

No doubt the single source which has been most quoted and which
most complicates an accurate appraisal of Philip Marlowe is Chandler's own essay "The Simple Art of Murder." The piece first appeared in the *Atlantic Monthly* in 1944 and, in a slightly revised
form, in the *Saturday Review of Literature* in 1950. Since then,
it has become a favorite of anthologists. In those oft-quoted phrases,
Chandler wrote:

> In everything that can be called art there is a quality of re-
> demption. . . . down these mean streets a man must go who is
> not himself mean, who is neither tarnished nor afraid. The de-
> tective in this kind of story must be such a man. He is the hero;
> he is everything. He must be a complete man and a common
> man and yet an unusual man. . . .
> He is a lonely man and his pride is that you will treat him as
> a proud man or be very sorry you ever saw him. He talks as the
> man of his age talks—that is, with rude wit, a lively sense of the
> grotesque, a disgust for sham, and a contempt for pettiness.
> The story is this man's adventure in search of a hidden truth,

> . . . If there were enough like him, the world would be a very
> safe place to live in, without becoming too dull to be worth
> living in.

Surely, Philip Marlowe is a man of wit and honor, a common yet
unusual man, a lonely and proud man, and even, in a sense, a "man
of his age." But to say he is a "complete man" and that *because*
he is the hero he is *everything* is a hyperbole that demands some
qualification.

Ross Macdonald is one who has legitimately objected to this
characterization. He comments that, "While there may be 'a quality
of redemption' in a good novel, it belongs to the whole work and
is not the private property of one of the characters. . . . The
detective-as-redeemer is a backward step in the direction of sentimental romance, and an over-simplified world of good guys and
bad guys." If we take "The Simple Art of Murder" at its face value,
Macdonald's remark is a significant criticism.

But Chandler's comments elsewhere suggest that he was not
unaware of his own tendency to exaggeration. In a 1946 letter to
Howard Haycraft, for example, he cautioned: "You must not take
a polemic piece of writing like my own article from the *Atlantic*
too literally. I could have written a piece of propaganda in favor
of the English detective story [which he despised] just as easily.
All polemic writing is overstated."

Thus, despite its magisterial tone and popularity, "The Simple
Art of Murder" is obviously not the place to begin an effort to
understand Philip Marlowe. More to the point are Chandler's letters
where he was much more direct about Marlowe and his relationship to him. In a 1951 letter, for instance, he warned: "You must
remember that Marlowe is not a real person. He is a creature of
fantasy. He is in a false position because I put him there." While
it may seem unnecessary to call attention to the fact that a fictional
character is a "creature of fantasy in a false position," some balance
to the apotheosis of the detective in "The Simple Art of Murder"
must be struck. And Chandler's comment correctly directs us to the
works themselves, to the "fantasies" and to Marlowe's "false position" in them for accurate assessment of this enigmatic character.

Our first interest no doubt is in the "facts" about this man.
But a close examination of the novels reveals that there are pre-

cious few. We know that in *The Big Sleep* he is thirty-three years old and fifteen years later, in *The Long Goodbye*, he is forty-two. We know that he is six feet tall, weighs 190 pounds, smokes both pipes and cigarettes (which he lights with kitchen matches), and drinks (almost anything but sweet drinks) openly and without hesitation—though Chandler resented the suggestion that he was "always full of whiskey." Cary Grant was the actor who most resembled Marlowe to Chandler's mind, but he was also much impressed by Humphrey Bogart's portrayal in the original film version of *The Big Sleep*.

When Howard Spencer prompts him in *The Long Goodbye* to "tell me a little about yourself, Mr. Marlowe," we get a rare, and cryptic, autobiographical sketch:

> I'm a licensed private investigator and have been for quite a while. I'm a lone wolf, unmarried, getting middle-aged and not rich. I've been in jail more than once and I don't do divorce business. I like liquor and women and chess and a few other things. . . . I'm a native son, born in Santa Rosa, both parents dead, no brothers or sisters, and when I get knocked off in a dark alley sometime, if it happens, . . . nobody will feel that the bottom has dropped out of his or her life.

In *The Big Sleep*, he tells General Sternwood that he "went to college once and can still speak English if there's any demand for it. There isn't much in my trade. I worked for Mr. Wilde, the District Attorney, as an investigator once. . . . I was fired. For insubordination. I test very high on insubordination, General." His college education was evidently sufficient to allow him to toss about literary references to such authors as Hemingway, Flaubert, and T. S. Eliot, and in *Farewell, My Lovely* he comments on Lindsay Marriott's "nice use of the subjunctive mood."

Marlowe is seldom at home in the novels and even when he is we get little description of his private surroundings. In *The Big Sleep*, he lives in a small apartment in the Hobart Arms on Franklin Avenue which he describes briefly as "the room I had to live in. It was all I had in the way of a home. In it was everything that was mine, that had any association for me, any past, anything that took the place of family. Not much; a few books, pictures, radio, chessmen, old letters, stuff like that. Nothing."

By the later novels he has moved to "a house on Yucca Avenue
in the Laurel Canyon district. It was a small hillside house on a
dead-end street with a long flight of redwood steps to the front
door and a grove of eucalyptus trees across the way. It was furnished. . . . The rent was low. . . ." And that is about all the physical
description we ever get of the place. Home, for Marlowe, is largely
a place to sleep, a place to puzzle over chess problems when he
can't sleep, and a place for breakfast. Breakfast is something of a
ritual for him. It generally consists of several cups of black coffee
(he is quite proud of his coffee-making), eggs (frequently soft-
boiled), toast, and honey—all consumed while poring over the morning papers. Other meals are eaten out and frequently consist of a
sandwich and martini or Gibson.

He spends relatively more time at his office, often simply waiting, and we get a considerably more detailed description of those
environs. In one of the few inconsistencies which Chandler allowed
in the novels, the office is described on the *seventh* floor in *The
Big Sleep* and on the *sixth* floor in novels thereafter. But it is
obviously the same office in the Cahuenga Building on Hollywood
Boulevard near Ivar. The fairly tight space is divided into a small,
outer reception room and a slightly larger inner office, his "thinking parlor." The reception room is described in *The Big Sleep* in
terms of the reaction of a client who wrinkles her nose "at the
faded red settee, the two odd semi-easy chairs, the net curtains that
needed laundering and the boy's size library table with the vener-
able magazines on it to give the place a professional touch." The
inner office contains:

> a rust-red carpet, not very young, five green filing cases, three
> of them full of California climate, an advertising calendar show-
> ing the Quints rolling around on a sky-blue floor, in pink dresses,
> with seal-brown hair and sharp black eyes as large as mammoth
> prunes. There were three near-walnut chairs, the usual desk
> with the usual blotter, penset, ashtray and telephone, and the
> usual squeaky swivel-chair behind it.

One of the desk drawers contains his "office bottle" and pony
glasses, and a few more details of the place appear as the novels
progress. In *The High Window*, for example, a glass top appears for

the desk, as well as "a framed license bond for the wall, . . . a wash-
bowl in a stained wood cupboard, a hat-rack, . . . and two open
windows with net curtains that puckered in and out like the lips
of a toothless old man sleeping. The same stuff I had had last year,
and year before that. Not beautiful, not gay, but better than a tent
on the beach."

When out of the office, Marlowe, like most Californians, is a
creature of the automobile. He likes big cars, primarily Oldsmobiles
and Chryslers, and has a penchant for convertibles; when it rains,
the convertibles usually leak.

But finally all these bits of information do little to illumine the
character of Philip Marlowe. One observer, Russell Davies, has even
suggested that Marlowe's "strength," the quality which makes him
an "interestingly perplexing character . . . , paradoxically, is that he
is in some ways more like a literal nonentity" than any of his
contemporaries. Marlowe is finally not so much a fully developed
character as he is an attitude, a tone of voice. And, as Clive James
has argued, it is a voice with which a reader can readily identify,
"day-dreaming of being tough, of defending the innocent, of being
the hero."

Part of the appeal of that voice is its powerful projection of the
difference between the way things *are* and the way they *should be*.
And the resulting tensions created by that dual mind control Marlowe's reactions to events, temper his relations with other characters, and are finally his own undoing.

His dualistic approach to other characters tends to divide them
into victims and victimizers. His idealistic sensibilities draw him
spontaneously and sympathetically to the down-trodden, to characters like Merle Davis and Terry Lennox. He has open and ready
contempt, on the other hand, for the societal powers responsible
for their plights—the Elizabeth Murdocks, the Harlan Potters, the
corrupt Bay City Police, etc. But even as Marlowe is quick to de-
fend whomever he perceives as helpless, so is he—more often than
not—disappointed in the results of his own well-intentioned hero-
ics. The world, and other people, simply refuse to conform to his
high principles. The typical end of a Marlowe novel finds him dis-
illusioned, drinking or playing chess or both, and unable to assimilate the meaning of his case or of his own role in it. Most bleakly
in *The Long Goodbye*, the final pages leave him listening to fading

footsteps, unable to comprehend how the world could have sunk—
so unexpectedly—to such depths of dishonesty.

The primary exception to this pattern, *Playback*, while it seems
to offer consolation, is really only a momentary and fated swing to
the opposite extreme. Marlowe is, at first, his usual despondent,
isolated self: "wherever I went, whatever I did, this was what I
would come back to. A blank wall in a meaningless room in a
meaningless house." But his gloomy reflections are interrupted by
a phone call from Linda Loring who proposes marriage. Suddenly,
the "air was full of music." But, even though this upbeat attitude
spills over into *The Poodle Springs Story*, the fragment which
Chandler began just before his death, the marks of disillusionment
are on the wall there too, anticipating the usual reversal.

Marlowe's dualism of mind, his split between an idealistic longing and an imperfect present, also colors his sexual relationships,
and those relationships can assist us in better understanding this
captivating voice. But first, it is perhaps appropriate to attempt to
sort out the confusion that has arisen in this regard from some of
the popular criticism which has taken great pleasure in declaring
Marlowe homosexual. One critic, Michael Mason, for example, points
to Marlowe's "mixture of tenderness and boyish admiration" for
Moose Malloy (in *Farewell, My Lovely*) and calls it "morally ob-
tuse." In the same novel, he calls disparaging attention to this
description of Red Norgaard:

> His voice was soft, dreamy, so delicate for a big man that it
> was startling. It made me think of another soft-voiced big man
> [Moose Malloy] I had strangely liked. . . . He had the eyes you
> never see, that you only read about. Violet eyes. Eyes like a girl.
> His skin was as soft as silk. Lightly reddened, but it would
> never tan.

Another critic, Gershon Legman, has made the most famous indict-
ment of this passage, saying:

> No matter how 'strangely' Chandler's detective, Marlowe, moons
> over these big men, they are always beating him up. . . . The
> true explanation of Marlowe's temperamental disinterest in
> women is not 'honour,' but his interest in men. . . . Chandler's

> Marlowe is clearly homosexual—a butterfly, as the Chinese say,
> dreaming that he is a man.

But here there is a certain straying from the facts. Although one's
perception of what exactly constitutes "mooning" may be subjective, it is demonstrable that Marlowe is never beaten up by either
of the "big men" referred to here (Moose and Red). The implied
substitution of physical beatings for sexual gratification simply is not
a part of the novels. Neither is Marlowe exactly "disinterested" in
women, as his own remarks and actions and the proposal of marriage in *Playback* demonstrate. Among the facts which Legman
overlooks are that Red is, like Marlowe, a former policeman, that
his assistance is instrumental in Marlowe's resolution of the case,
and the two, therefore, have adequate basis for a relationship
without the implications of sexual attraction. Similarly, Marlowe's
fascination with Moose, despite his rather uncontrollable violence,
stems from the bizarre manner in which they first meet and from
his conviction that Moose is only a pawn in some larger game. But
perhaps the best comment on the subject was Chandler's own: "Mr.
Legman seems to me to belong to that rather numerous class of
American neurotics which cannot conceive of a close friendship between a couple of men as other than homosexual."

Marlowe does, in a real sense, idealize his big men. But to
construe that admiration as homosexual lust is to misconstrue an
essential facet of Marlowe's character. There is in Marlowe a strong
tendency to idealize everything, a tendency most obvious in his
relationships with women and one which has also garnered him
considerable unwarranted criticism on that subject.

At the greatest extreme, Chandler has been accused, by Geoffrey Hartmann, of indulging (through Marlowe) in "conventional
woman hating," and Michael Mason has argued that the novels'
"moral scheme is in truth pathologically harsh on women, and
pathologically lenient towards men." While neither of these assessments is strictly supportable, they do call attention to Marlowe's
difficulties in relating to the opposite sex, a subject which demands
scrutiny if we are to fully appreciate Chandler's detective. We
should focus first, no doubt, on some of the specific scenes which
have occasioned most of the criticism.

One such scene occurs in *The Big Sleep*. Marlowe returns to his apartment, after a long, hard day, to find Carmen Sternwood lying in his bed nude and giggling. After a long exchange in which he tries, at first gently and then more threateningly, to persuade her to leave, she finally dresses and departs. As Marlowe hears the elevator descend, he tells us:

> I walked to the windows and pulled the shades up and opened the windows wide. The night air came drifting in with a kind of stale sweetness that still remembered automobile exhausts and the streets of the city. I reached for my drink and drank it slowly. The apartment house door closed itself down below me. . . . I went back to the bed and looked down at it. The imprint of her head was still in the pillow, of her small corrupt body still on the sheets.
>
> I put my empty glass down and tore the bed to pieces savagely.

Taken out of context, Marlowe's actions indeed seem rather excessive. And, to further extract quotes from context, it is possible to make a rather damaging case against Marlowe by recalling his thoughts during this encounter with Carmen: "It's so hard for women—even nice women—to realize that their bodies are not irresistible"; or by pointing out his remark of the next morning, "You can have a hangover from other things than alcohol. I had one from women. Women made me sick."

Considered in isolation, as they often are, these remarks do suggest a man with a revulsion for the opposite sex. But such an interpretation neglects the circumstances surrounding the scene. Just prior to his encounter with Carmen, Marlowe has come from one roughly parallel with Carmen's sister Vivian, who has also attempted to use her sexuality on him to extract the information and cooperation she desires. And this is not the first time Marlowe has found Carmen nude and up to her own games of sexual coercion. She has, in fact, been throwing herself at him ever since he walked into the door of the Sternwood mansion in Chapter 1. And finally, it is at about this point, halfway through the novel, that Marlowe is beginning to perceive that this sort of sexual gamesmanship was at the root of one of the book's essential puzzles, the disappearance of Rusty Regan. At the end, of course, his suspicions prove absolutely accurate.

Though the novel does derive a certain amount of its tension from the strife between the sexes, it is an oversimplification to call this "conventional woman hating." Marlowe does, in fact, develop a certain sympathy for Carmen at the novel's end where he dares to suggest that "she might even get herself cured."

But, while we can not legitimately accuse Marlowe of a general misogyny, it is true that his relationships with women are often strained. A major part of his problem derives from the woman-on-a-pedestal syndrome which is historically associated with Marlowe's kind of knight-errantry. Take *Farewell, My Lovely,* for example. Anne Riordan in that book (and later in "The Pencil") is one of Chandler's strongest, most independent, most likeable female characters. Marlowe is clearly taken with her and, in one of Chandler's purpler passages, he lets go of her hand "slowly as you let go of a dream when you wake with the sun in your face and have been in an enchanted valley." But in what he calls "one of my rare moments of delicacy," Marlowe refuses her offer of overnight accommodations. Later, he comments to Lt. Randall: "She's a nice girl. Not my type. . . . I like smooth shiny girls, hardboiled and loaded with sin." At least partly, the statement is simply an attempt at a macho camaraderie with the Lieutenant. But it also suggests a desire to keep his relationship with Riordan on a distant, impersonal level, unsullied by a contemptible reality—to keep her on a pedestal "in an enchanted valley." So far as we know, Marlowe never has anything to do with "shiny, hardboiled" girls.

Of course, another reason why Marlowe can't become involved with a woman is that such romantic subplots tend to detract from the main story. Such single-mindedness is evident, indeed, in almost any other writer of mystery novels. Traditionally, the isolation of the detective-protagonist is endemic to the form itself, an unavoidable occupational hazard. And only in *The Poodle Springs Story* did Chandler himself attempt to break with that mold.

But, aside from this formal consideration, Marlowe's attitude toward women reflects the same conflict between his idealism and his experience which colors all his actions. A part of him longs for the perfect goddess; his experience persistently shatters that

dream. When he thinks he has found a person close to his ideal in
Anne Riordan, his impulse is to enshrine her. In *The Long Goodbye,* Marlowe appears to manage his most reasonable perspective
on male-female relationships, but, even there, traces of his dualism
persist. One bit of dialogue on the subject of women occurs early
in the book between Marlowe and Terry Lennox. When Lennox
begins to rail about "the goddam women . . . waving their hands
and screwing up their faces and tinkling their goddam bracelets
and making with the packaged charm," Marlowe counters with,
"Take it easy. . . . So they're human. . . . What did you expect—
golden butterflies hovering in a rosy mist?" Marlowe here demonstrates his own awareness of the absurdity of expecting women to
be other than what they are—human. But by the end of the novel,
when he has been thoroughly disgusted by Eileen Wade and her
court performance following her husband's death, Marlowe is also
capable of deriving a certain pleasure from the "rude sign" over
the "corn-beef joint" where he stops to eat which reads: "Men Only.
Dogs and Women Not Admitted."

In the first exchange with Lennox, Marlowe appears to acknowl-
edge the flaws of an excessively idealistic approach to the opposite
sex; women are not, in fact, "butterflies . . . in a rosy mist." In the
second example, he recognizes, despite his pleasure, that it is a
"rude sign," that is, ill-mannered and discourteous, thus implicitly
acknowledging the flaws of the contemptuous side of his personality.
But though he has these scenes of quasi-recognition, he fails to act
on them productively. He continues, in the manner of his age, to
respond to women in terms of stereotypes. Marlowe is no woman
hater, but neither is he totally isolated from the general misogynis-
tic tendencies of the one-dimensional, patriarchal world in which
he operates.

To this point, we have spent considerable time arguing what
Marlowe is not. Ironically, Russell Davies has suggested that "Marlowe is more easily defined by what he will not do than by what he
will." Actually, this kind of negative definition fits perfectly with
the romance tradition from which Marlowe springs. In Chandler's
very first short story he called his detective Mallory, in likely reference to Sir Thomas Malory's *Morte Darthur* (1485), one of the
prototypes of the knightly romance. In that early work, the king's
orders to his knights are that they are

> never to do outragiousity nor murder, and always to flee trea-
> son; also, by no means to be cruel, but to give mercy unto him
> that asketh mercy . . . , and always to do ladies, damosels, and
> gentlewomen succour, upon pain of death. Also that no man
> take no battles in a wrongful quarrel for no law, nor for no
> world's goods.

These negatively expressed principles are a fair summation of Marlowe's code. His disappointment, and his despair, finally, is that
the code of honor from which his motivations derive appears no
longer valid in the world in which he finds himself. Marlowe's noble, but dated, sensibilities are a part of the "false position" in
which Chandler places him. And it is a part of Chandler's theme
that a man of such sensibilities has, regrettably, become an anach-
ronism in the modern world.

That notion is most clearly explicated in *The Long Goodbye*.
In that work, Marlowe is at first enamored of Lennox's apparent
Englishness. His "Old World" accent and manners are taken, initially, as a hopeful sign of the possibility of the continuation of
chivalry in the New World. But ultimately it is proven to be only
a façade. Lennox is as dissolute and "New World" as any of Chandler's characters. And, as Natasha Spender has observed, Lennox is
one of the three obvious self-portraits Chandler included in that
book. At the end of *The Long Goodbye,* then, we see two fictional-
ized parts of the Chandler character in confrontation. And that confrontation recalls another work which Marlowe's name echoes.

That work is Joseph Conrad's *Heart of Darkness*. In it, Conrad's Marlow is the detective-narrator in pursuit of the enigmatic
Mr. Kurtz and, as Max Byrd has pointed out, "What Marlow discovers, ironically, is the kind of man he himself is, his kinship to
Kurtz, their indissoluble human connection. . . . everything in the
story cries out at us, after all, that Kurtz and Marlow are one person, two parts of a single entity." Much the same can be said for
the relationship between Terry Lennox and Chandler's Marlowe in
*The Long Goodbye*. But, though Chandler's Marlowe may sense
his "indissoluble human connection" with Lennox, his response is
to deny it, to berate him for being "a moral defeatist," and to continue to hold himself apart, in sadly desperate isolation, holding
out for his rigid, noble, archaic code.

Such behavior is at once Marlowe's strength and his weakness. To the end, he remains, as he himself puts it, "a romantic. . . . I hear voices crying in the night and I go see what's the matter." His weakness is that his romantic notions and motivations never alter or mature, never allow him the deeper insights into the human dilemma of a character like Conrad's Marlow. His strength and no doubt a source of much of his popularity lies in his very rigidity, his adherence to principle above all else. But he is never able to achieve an understanding of himself as operating within a fallen world, and that is his major failing as a modern hero. And yet he remains an appealing *voice*. Part of that appeal, no doubt, lies in his audience's identification with his tough, unswerving idealism. And it is in that sense that he is a "man of his age" and, indeed, a commentary on his age. But the appeal of that voice is also a product of its language and style, and that is the subject of our next chapter.

# 7

## Beyond Formula: Raymond Chandler's Style

> "My whole career is based on the idea that the formula doesn't matter, the thing that counts is what you do with the formula; that is to say, it is a matter of style."
>
> *Letter, March 18, 1948*

Chandler once suggested that there were only two kinds of writers, "writers who write stories and writers who write writing," and he clearly intended to include himself in the latter group. For Chandler, stories (or plots), particularly as developed in detective novels, were little more than an artificial puzzle promising the reader a neatly turned resolution within a few hundred pages read. His own intent was considerably less formulaic. He was not interested in merely constructing distracting tales. Instead, he was intrigued by the possibility of using this popular form to impress some markedly subtler notions on an audience which typically saw itself concerned only with escape.

As he once expressed his intentions, "From the beginning, from the very first pulp story, it was always with me a question . . . of putting into the stuff something they [the readers] would not shy off from, perhaps even not know was there as a conscious realization, but which would somehow distill through their minds and leave an afterglow."

He elaborated this point more fully on another occasion: "The thing is to squeeze the last drop out of the medium you have learned to use. The aim is not essentially different from the aim of Greek tragedy, but we are dealing with a public that is only semi-literate and we have to make an art of a language they can understand." To forge an art from a common language was Chandler's fundamental ambition. And believing, as he did, that, "All language begins with speech, and the speech of the common man at that," it is hardly surprising that he saw the detective/mystery genre, at least at first, as a perfectly viable laboratory for experimenting with the very generation of language. As he said:

> All I wanted to do when I began writing was to play with a fascinating new language, to see what it would do as a means of expression which might remain on the level of unintellectual thinking and yet acquire the power to say things which are usually said only with a literary air. . . . I wrote melodrama because when I looked around me it was the only kind of writing I saw that was relatively honest and yet was not trying to put over somebody's party line.

Besides offering a popular medium, the choice of melodrama also helped Chandler sidestep two of his dominant aversions: politics and intellectualism.

Politics, politicians, and political ideologies were subjects about which he had few kind words throughout his life. He calls Sheriff Petersen, in *The Long Goodbye,* for example, "a living testimonial to the fact that you can hold an important public office forever in our country with no qualifications for it but a clean nose, a photogenic face, and a close mouth. If on top of that you look good on a horse, you are unbeatable." And on the subject of intellectualism, he once remarked, "Thinking in terms of ideas destroys the power to think in terms of emotions and sensations. I have at times a futile urge to explain to whoever will listen why it is that the whole apparatus of intellectualism bores me. But you have to use the language of intellectualism to do it. Which is the bunk."

Intellectualism, for Chandler, was a process of abstraction; politics, a process of manipulation. Neither offered much insight, except as subjects for ridicule, into the emotional aspects of human nature which were central to him. He was never bothered by having his works referred to as "melodramatic" or "sentimental"— terms of denigration in literary circles—because melodrama and sentimental romance were exactly right for his purposes for two reasons. First, they were the genres most widely accepted by the broad audience which he wished to reach, and, second, they were pure forms, clearly defined and unadulterated by any political or intellectual overlays.

In melodrama, our expectations are fixed; the black and white hats condition our responses. Chandler then can play on those expectations, frustrating them with stories which deny simple resolutions and which are couched in language that, while seeming common, always hints at deeper implications. Thus, the simplicity of the form freed Chandler, paradoxically, to complicate its medium, to charge a superficial puzzle with subtle undertones of emotion. It was the conveying of these emotional messages that Chandler considered his principal challenge.

But to deal with such ill-defined, nonintellectual forces, Chandler also knew, required a system of strict control. That system, which he devised as the regulator of his powerful style, was what he called his "objective method." It is a method by which he hoped to "render a state of mind . . . purely through the tone of the description," or, in other words, to conjure an emotional response strictly through the selection and presentation of objective details. He elaborated this method further in this story written to a friend:

> A long time ago when I was writing for the pulps I put into a story a line like 'He got out of the car and walked across the sun-drenched sidewalk until the shadow of the awning over the entrance fell across his face like the touch of cool water.' They took it out when they published the story. Their readers didn't appreciate this sort of thing—just held up the action.
>
> I set out to prove them wrong. My theory was that the readers just *thought* they cared about nothing but the action; that really, although they didn't know it, the thing they cared about, and that I cared about, was the creation of emotion through dialogue and description. The thing they remembered, that haunted them was not, for example, that a man got killed, but that in the moment of his death he was trying to pick a

paper clip up off the polished surface of a desk and it kept
slipping away from him, so that there was a look of strain on his
face and his mouth was half open in a kind of tormented grin,
and the last thing in the world he thought about was death. He
didn't even hear the knock on the door. That damn little paper
clip kept slipping away from his fingers.

This paper clip story deftly illustrates Chandler's notion of rendering "emotion through dialogue and description." Like most detective fiction, it concerns death, and it verges on melodrama. But
in its juxtaposition of the concrete detail of the paper clip—that
omnipresent and expendable trivia of the modern world—and the
grim, essential reality of death, the scene sharpens our awareness
of the tenuous fragility and absurdity of life. The man's fascination
becomes ours, and his "tormented grin" epitomizes his less than
rational, but recognizably human, response to this mysterious transformation. The scene evokes a deeply emotional response even
though the language strives hard not to be emotional, to stick
scrupulously to objective detail. But the choice of detail and the
precision of its use conveys a profound undercurrent of human
feelings and human futility—even while questioning its own assumptions of the possibility of objectivity.

This "objective method" is capable of functioning equally well
on a wide variety of subjects. Consider, for example, Marlowe's first
approach to the Grayle mansion in *Farewell, My Lovely*. After a
wrangle with the guard at the gate, Marlowe drives in and tells us:

The drive curved and tall molded hedges of dark green completely screened it from the street and from the house. Through
a green gate I saw a Jap gardener at work weeding a huge
lawn. He was pulling a piece of weed out of the vast velvet expanse and sneering at it. . . . Then the hedge ended in a wide
circle in which half a dozen cars were parked.

One of them was a small coupe. There were a couple of very
nice two-tone Buicks of the latest model, good enough to go for
the mail in. There was a black limousine, with dull nickel
louvres and hubcaps the size of bicycle wheels. . . .

Off to the left, beyond the parking space there was a sunken
garden with a fountain at each of the four corners. The en-

trance was barred by a wrought-iron gate with a flying Cupid in the middle. . . . There was an oblong pool with stone water-lilies in it and a big stone bullfrog sitting on one of the leaves. Still farther a rose colonnade led to a thing like an altar, hedged in at both sides, yet not so completely but that the sun lay in an arabesque along the steps of the altar. And far over to the left there was a wild garden, not very large, with a sun-dial in the corner near an angle of wall that was built to look like a ruin. And there were flowers. There were a million flowers.

The house itself was not so much. It was smaller than Buckingham Palace, rather gray for California, and probably had fewer windows than the Chrysler Building.

Perhaps the first thing that strikes us about this (and numerous similar passages in Chandler) is its slow, methodical, "objective" compilation of detail. But our second and almost simultaneous realization is surely that it is hardly objective. With its reliance on simple, declarative statements and catalogues of minutiae, the description creates an illusion of objectivity, but it requires little examination to discover that Marlowe's sensibilities considerably color both the selection of details and their characterization.

While it might be argued, as Frank MacShane does, that "Marlowe's personality affects the descriptions and compromises to some degree the 'objective method' Chandler believed in," it seems more likely that this bipolar tension is an indispensable component of the method. Russell Davies has remarked on Chandler and Marlowe's "splendid collusion in the texture of 'their' first-person narrative," and Ross Macdonald has observed further that "it is Marlowe's doubleness that makes him interesting: the hard-boiled mask half-concealing Chandler's poetic and satiric mind. Part of our pleasure derives from the interplay between the mind of Chandler and the voice of Marlowe."

That "interplay," that "splendid collusion," is quite apparent in the description of the Grayle mansion and grounds. True, we are only told about the drive, the lawn, the garage, the gardens, and the house. But that capitulation of "bare facts" obviously conceals a great deal more information. Significantly, for example, the hedges completely isolate the property from the outside world, and, even though they are sneered at, there are weeds in this "vast velvet expanse." Moreover, Marlowe obviously delights in describing the excessiveness of "nickel louvres and hubcaps the size of bicycle wheels" on the limousine, as well as in suggesting that the Buicks are "good enough to go for the mail in." And a particularly caustic irony underlies his observations that Cupid, the god of love, is barring the wrought iron gate, that the waterlilies as well as the bullfrog are lifeless stone, and that "a thing like an altar" and something "built to look like a ruin" have been constructed here to display the occupants' presumed taste, piety, and class. And lest there should be anything lacking, there are the obligatory "million flowers." The vulgar excess and artificiality of these details and what they imply about the self-indulgent modern world harp on one of Chandler's favorite themes.

The description of the Grayle estate is also significant for its pacing. Chandler's brilliant pacing in such descriptive scenes is often overlooked even though they frequently set up the gems of dialogue which are more commonly praised. In this case, a long, laborious description of the grounds is suddenly undercut by the stark brevity and gross imprecision of the description of the house itself: "smaller than Buckingham Palace . . . fewer windows than the Chrysler Building." The contempt which has been bubbling beneath the surface throughout Marlowe's comments on the lawn and garden suddenly strikes out with a vengeance, and the reader's attitude toward the property's inhabitants has been subtly shaped. As Chandler once remarked, "Marlowe and I do not despise the upper classes because they take baths and have money; we despise them because they are phoney." The phoniness which Marlowe has documented from the outside of the Grayle mansion has thoroughly prepared us for the phoniness we will encounter inside.

The manner of the description of the Grayle estate, especially in its sardonic last lines, owes a great deal of its bite, of course, to Marlowe's own style, particularly his peculiar brand of humor. And one of the appealing and paradoxical things about Chandler is that, despite the somberness of his tales, his books are very funny.

Some of Marlowe's wisecracks are virtually legendary. To Carmen Sternwood's "Tall, aren't you?" in the opening pages of *The Big Sleep*, for example, he responds "I didn't mean to be," and a pattern of witty repartee is established for the rest of the novels. Sometimes the wisecracks get much more elaborate. When Goble, in *Playback*, suggests "Me and you could get along . . . if you had any brains," Marlowe responds "And if you had any manners and were six inches taller and had a different face and another name and didn't act like you thought you could lick your weight in frog spawn." But whatever the complexity of the remarks, they serve a similar function; they are devices of control. Regardless of who is on the receiving end of one of these put-downs, he or she is invariably thrown off balance for a moment, forced to take another line of argument, or at least angered to the point of making an issue of Marlowe's manners. Whatever the specific case, Marlowe's quicker tongue gives him a certain power, even if only for an instant. In *The Big Sleep*, for example, his wry, one-word question "Finished?", after Canino has tried vainly to annihilate him, startles Canino just long enough for Marlowe to perform the necessary deed, his only killing in the novels.

Often Chandler's sense of humor and his fascination with language coalesce in some remarkable lines. In *The Big Sleep*, Harry Jones comments: "You know how it is. A guy's there and you see him and then he ain't there and you don't not see him until something makes you think of it." The sentence makes sense, if jarringly, and could certainly be improved grammatically by changing "you don't not see him until" to "you don't miss him until." But such "improvement" would totally obscure Chandler's point. This brief excursion into Harry Jones' awkward slang permits Chandler to set up a vivid exchange on the nature of language, specifically built around the distinction between presence and absence. In that sentence, we read "A guy's there . . . and then he ain't there" and "you see him . . . and you don't not see him." The grammar may be poor, but the balance is perfect. And the sense of that balanced, if slangy, construction is that while "presence" is obvious and visible, "absence" is more elusive; it is not "a thing"—it is something one thinks about only when reminded by something else. "Seeing" is our way of comprehending "present" things. It would seem then that "not seeing" might be a way of comprehending "absent" things. From an intellectual point of view, we know, of course, that such is not the case, that Harry has simply exceeded the bounds of intelligible language. But in that very fact lies Chandler's point—

that language is but a poor reflection of the complexity of which the mind is capable. And, paradoxically, even the language of Harry Jones can launch us beyond our normal perceptions simply by disregarding our learned expectations. The effect is a vivid example of the evocative power of Chandler's seemingly offhand prose.

Chandler was keenly interested in slang throughout his life and claimed that "there are only two kinds that are any good: slang that has established itself in the language, and slang that you make up yourself. Everything else is apt to be passé before it gets into print." Much of Chandler's slang was of the "made up" variety—made up, but closely based on the rhythms of street language. He was particularly pleased that Eugene O'Neill used the term "the big sleep" as a synonym for death in his *The Iceman Cometh* (written in 1939) as if it were accepted slang; but Chandler claimed he'd invented it himself. His remarkable inventiveness is apparent in most of the passages which pass for authentic slang. For example, in *The Long Goodbye*, Mendy Menendez regales Marlowe with the lines, "I'm a big bad man, Marlowe. I make lots of dough. I got to make lots of dough to juice the guys I got to juice in order to make lots of dough to juice the guys I got to juice." In its peculiarly circular logic, the statement is at once farcical and tragic. Its humor derives from its rhythmical, inane repetition; its sadness from the self-perpetuating moral emptiness which it only thinly veils. And, though its cadence has the feel of the streets, its word play and rhythm manifest a conscious craftsmanship.

In the early novels, in particular, Chandler's meticulous craftsmanship is more conspicuous and, thus, more easily studied. In the later novels, his techniques are less obtrusive. *The High Window*, for example, is laden with the mannerism of repetition, a device which doubtless owes something to Ernest Hemingway. This paragraph, with its eight repetitions of the word *and* appears early in the novel:

> In and around the old houses there are flyblown restaurants and Italian fruitstands and cheap apartment houses and little candy stores where you can buy even nastier things than their candy. And there are ratty hotels where nobody except people named Smith and Jones sign the register and where the night clerk is half watchdog and half pander.

The paragraph is an excerpt from a lengthier description of Bunker Hill, a section of town fallen from a former splendor into a general and pervasive decay. The nouns (houses, restaurants, fruitstands, apartment houses, candy stores, hotels) suggest a thriving community. The adjectives (old, flyblown, cheap, ratty) imply the demise of that community. And the vague suggestions about the "nastier things" available at the candy store and the guarded anonymity in which people live here hint at a more intrinsic decay. Stringing all this information together with the simple repetition of *and* tends to equalize each element; the result is an air of objectivity even as Chandler overlays a subjective veneer which conditions his reader's response.

Often Chandler uses a similar kind of repetitive device to comment on the inherent weaknesses of another element of this California society. When we first meet Lois Magic in *The High Window*, for example, we are told that:

> Her mouth was too wide, her eyes were too blue, her makeup was too vivid. . . .
> She wore white duck slacks, blue and white open-toed sandals over bare feet and crimson toenails, a white silk blouse and a necklace of green stones that were not square cut emeralds. Her hair was as artificial as a night club lobby.
> On the chair beside her there was a white straw garden hat with a brim the size of a spare tire and a white satin chin strap. On the brim of the hat lay a pair of green sun glasses with lenses the size of doughnuts.

The initial repetition of the word *too* suggests the general excess which marks the extreme personal indulgence at the root of this society. That excess is echoed in the description of Lois' oversized hat brim and sunglasses. And such repetition, particularly of the word *too,* is one of Chandler's favorite devices for conveying a sense of the society's general dissipation.

Another typically Chandlerian feature of this passage is its reliance on color to convey emotional tone. The dominant color here is white and the word is repeated five times in a very short space. Though Lois Magic may have blue eyes, a bit of blue on her shoes, crimson toenails, a fake green necklace and green sunglasses, she is essentially a stark, colorless vision. Many of Chandler's characters share this starkness. Typically, they are dressed in white, or black, or black and white, or gray, or brown—lacking any but the merest hint of vivid colors. The consistency of this device suggests a certain implicit thematic intent: obviously these people are without vitality. They are, to borrow Chandler's simile, "as artificial as a night club lobby."

And similes, of course, are another of Chandler's well-known mannerisms, virtually a trademark. He once remarked that the purpose of the simile is to "convey at once a simple visual image." Similes like "as stiff as a breadstick," "a hand like a wood rasp," "as bald as a grapefruit," and "eyes like holes poked in a snowbank" stick fairly strictly to the "simple visual image" dictum. But Chandler is most inventive when he stretches his own rule to include senses beyond the visual, when he uses the simile to elicit emotion, when he yokes seemingly disparate notions for their humor or shock value, when he extends the simile to a device for social comment, or when he strings similes together for their sheer poetry.

Phrases like "lonely as lighthouses," for example, or "soundless as shadows on grass" or "as calm as an adobe wall in the moonlight" still retain a visual connection. But they also allude to the sense of hearing, in the second example, and appeal to the emotions in the other two. This emotional appeal is also evident in similes like "as anonymous as a nickel in a parking meter" which is simple and visual, but which also suggests the isolation and alienating anonymity which afflicts many of Chandler's characters.

But Chandler is most recognizable in similes like "as flustered as a side of beef" and "as restful as a split lip." The most famous of these unexpected comparisons is Marlowe's pronouncement that Moose Malloy is "about as inconspicuous as a tarantula on a slice of angel food." This yoking of such startlingly incongruous terms is at once a source of humor and an attempt to seek the limits of a concept: "as flustered as a side of beef" is about as little as one can be flustered; "as restful as a split lip" is obviously not very restful, nor is a tarantula likely to be overlooked on angel food. In any case, our sense of the limits of likeness exercises our sense of humor.

Occasionally, Chandler's use of the simile expands to include tacit social commentary. To say that a voice "faded off into a sort of sad whisper, like a mortician asking for a down payment," to describe Mrs. Murdock as "looking as unperturbed as a bank president refusing a loan," or to say that Elisha Morningstar "lifted his hands off the desk and made a steeple of the fingers, like an old time family lawyer getting set for a little tangled grammar," is to imply something decidedly negative about morticians, bank presidents, and lawyers. Apparently, such functionaries who maintain the legal system, oversee the economic system, and treat death as a profit-making industry are not Chandler's idea of the noble of the species. They are instead associated with the self-aggrandizing, alienating, lifeless forces which characterize the inhumanity of Chandler's landscapes. And anyone who seeks social comment in Chandler's works will find it primarily in such between-the-lines places. As we will see in the following chapter, such themes are seldom explicit in the novels.

Chandler's artful use of the simile is seldom without a certain self-consciousness and that obvious self-consciousness can enlighten the love-hate relationship which characterized his approach to writing throughout his career. For example, as Marlowe is coming out of a drugged state in *The Little Sister,* he comments, "I was as dizzy as a dervish, as weak as a worn-out washer, as low as a badger's belly, as timid as a titmouse, and as unlikely to succeed as a ballet dancer with a wooden leg." The piling up of similes here is appropriate to Marlowe's drugged state of mind, but it also exemplifies Chandler reveling in his own art. The initial similes in the string border on cliché with their persistent alliteration and iambic rhythms. But their very triteness and silly humor set us up for the unexpected, self-mocking final simile which lumbers along much like the image it describes; "a ballet dancer with a wooden leg."

Chandler's most self-conscious use of the simile occurs—with a quite different tone—in Roger Wade's typed notes in *The Long Goodbye,* which Marlowe reads:

> The moon's four days off the full and there's a square patch of moonlight on the wall and it's looking at me like a big blind milky eye, a wall eye. Joke. Goddam silly simile. Writers. Every-

thing has to be like something else. My head is as fluffy as
whipped cream but not as sweet. More similes. I could vomit
just thinking about the lousy racket.

The passage reflects the despondent side of the writer's self-consciousness about the tricks of his trade. After a lyrically alliterative
opening—"the moon's four days off the full"—the description quickly
degenerates to grotesquery and the writer's contemptuous inter-
ruption to call attention to the joke of the simile, but also of the
silliness of the whole enterprise of writing, of making everything
"like something else." The self-conscious contempt echoes in the
broken syntax and in the strained image "my head is as fluffy as
whipped cream but not as sweet." Wade's frustration is transpar-
ently Chandler's. He, too, feared that he might be wasting his talent
on a "lousy racket" and was determined, through his manipulation
of style, to make of it a genre as capable of meaning as any other.

Further insight into Chandler's use of style is suggested by
the statements of two contemporary critics. Richard Poirier, in his
book *A World Elsewhere: The Place of Style in American Literature,* has commented that, "The great works of American literature
are alive with the effort to stabilize certain feelings and attitudes
that have, as it were, no place in the world, no place at all except
where a writer's style can give them one." And Clive James has
asserted, with particular reference to Chandler, that "the secret of
plausibility lies in the style, and the secret of the style lies in
Marlowe's personality. Chandler once said that he thought of Marlowe as the American mind."

On one level, the "feelings and attitudes" which Chandler seeks
"to stabilize" are related to certain peculiarly American notions. In
a country as young and large as America, the vision of absolute
individual freedom lingers on. For a man of Marlowe's sensibilities,
the notion is balanced by a demand for absolute individual responsibility. The difficulty, for society and for Marlowe, arises when
the two ideas are dissociated, when freedom is exercised without
responsibility. Chandler's novels, not to mention the daily news,
are chronicles of such irresponsible freedom. And the abject frustration which Marlowe experiences in trying to resolve the problems
of the novels is the frustration of the American mind attempting

to come to grips with the obvious failure of its noble ideal of freedom.

On another level, the feelings and attitudes which Chandler seeks to stabilize are those of the writer in constant conflict with his own craft. This aspect of the novels is most readily apparent, of course, in *The Long Goodbye* where the novelist Roger Wade provides Chandler a forum for discussing the writer's difficulties. Much as the individual is torn by the freedom-responsibility problem, the writer is perpetually caught between his responsibility to represent the human dilemma authentically and his desire (and freedom) to be popular, to make money. Both Chandler and Roger Wade recognize and attempt to resolve the problem. And it is through the style in which the attempt is made that Chandler's own uniqueness emerges.

For example, early in *The Long Goodbye*, Marlowe is having a sleepless night following the receipt of Terry Lennox's letter raising questions about his own demise. Marlowe has an appointment the next morning with Howard Spencer, Roger Wade's literary agent. At 3 A.M. he is walking the floor, thinking:

> If it hadn't been for Mr. Howard Spencer at the Ritz-Beverly I would have killed a bottle and knocked myself out. And the next time I saw a polite character drunk in a Rolls-Royce Silver Wraith, I would depart rapidly in several directions. There is no trap so deadly as the trap you set for yourself.

That last sentence, by itself, has a dull, moralistic ring about it. But, in context, its flatness is tempered by the incongruity of the line which precedes it: "next time . . . I would depart rapidly in several directions." And that bit of humor is itself set up by the illusion of objectivity established by the careful inclusion of the full proper names of the agent, the hotel, and the automobile. Such deft mixing of the subjective and the objective, the humorous and the serious is characteristic of the Chandlerian style. But what is more significant for our discussion is the double context of that last sentence and the light it sheds on the writer's relationship to his craft.

On the one hand, the comment expresses Marlowe's outrage at

having been trapped by his own code. Terry Lennox, after all, did not seek Marlowe out; it was Marlowe's own helpfulness which drew him into this other man's story. But the statement's absolute tone also invites a broader application—to our own lives and to Chandler's as well. For Chandler, the "trap" he "set for himself" was the novels themselves. Throughout his life, his statements about his work followed two lines. He was alternately pleased by his experimentation in a slighted genre and concerned that the whole enterprise might be a grand waste of time. That dual pull between commitment and contempt, evident in his own life and work, is reflected in Marlowe and in other characters, like Roger Wade.

A slightly more hopeful example of this fundamental tension between optimism and despair also occurs in *The Long Goodbye*. Marlowe has been brought to the homicide division for interrogation. He tells us:

> The homicide skipper that year was a Captain Gregorius, a type of copper that is getting rarer but by no means extinct, the kind that solves crimes with the bright light, the soft sap, the kick to the kidneys, the knee to the groin, the fist to the solar plexus, the night stick to the base of the spine. Six months later he was indicted for perjury before a grand jury, booted without trial, and later stamped to death by a big stallion on his ranch in Wyoming.

The paragraph is both humorous and sharply ironic. Despite the vicious tactics of the homicide skipper, it would appear that, indeed, there is hope, macabre though it may be, for justice on a grand scale; it is perhaps particularly fitting that a man of such macho proclivities should be "stamped to death by a big stallion." But even that promise of a future justice is undercut in the very next paragraph. "Right now," Marlowe says, "I was his raw meat." Always there is the double pull—between a hope for a just future and the reality of an unjust present, between a commitment to others and a desire to withdraw from that commitment, between writing as noble endeavor and writing as self-set trap, between Marlowe's personal code and the impersonal world in which he must operate, between idealism and contempt. That the doubleness is elaborated within the confines of the detective novel is a tribute to the superior skills and unique vision of Raymond Chandler. Some critics, after all, have gone so far as to assert with George Elliott that, "there is no use pretending that the detective story has much to recommend it as a form. . . . no novel written within its conventions could be first-rate." But Richard Poirier, with a somewhat more open mind, has suggested alternatively that:

> The crucial problem for the best American writers is to evade all such categorizations [romance, melodrama, myth, realism, naturalism, mystery, etc.] and to find a language that will at once express and protect states of consciousness that cannot adequately be defined by conventional formulations. . . . Once beyond the superficiality of genre criticism and the limitations of other more sophisticated categorizations, what is most interesting in American literature is the attempt to 'build a world' wherein, say, even drunkenness might be the rule of the day.

Raymond Chandler has built a world in which even a dated knight-errantry, burlesqued by Marlowe's own self-deflating wit, is "the rule of the day." And to comprehend that world is to comprehend its author's literary ambitions as well as the events which shaped his life. Those biographical events have been covered in Chapter 1; and Chandler's intentions have been hinted at throughout this chapter.

He was explicit about those ambitions on only rare occasions. Once he wrote that "it is the dream of every . . . writer who is not a hopeless hack . . . to exceed the limits of a formula without destroying it." And in an introduction to a volume of his short stories, he wrote:

> The mystery story is a kind of writing that need not dwell in the shadow of the past and owes little if any allegiance to the cult of the classics . . . . There are no 'classics' of crime and detection. Not one. Within its frame of reference, which is the only way it should be judged, a classic is a piece of writing which exhausts the possibilities of its form and can hardly be surpassed. No story or novel of mystery has done that yet. Few have come close. Which is one of the principal reasons why otherwise reasonable people continue to assault the citadel.

Even while denying "any allegiance to the cult of the classics," he professes his own urge to write one. Even while demanding that a work be judged "within its frame of reference," he is driven to "exceed the limits" of that frame. Always there is the contradiction. Contradiction, of course, is not unusual among distinguished writers. What generally distinguishes them is their ability to control that contradictory vision, to explore all its ramifications equally.

For Chandler, the control is achieved through the tone of Philip Marlowe's voice and through a ceaseless language play which is always full of implications beyond the obvious. Which is to say, it is a matter of style.

# 8

---

# Purity and Perversity: The Vision of Raymond Chandler

"Why is it that Americans—of all people the quickest to reverse their moods—do not see the burlesque in my kind of writing?"

*Letter, March 1949*

Raymond Chandler was so committed to being a "writer of writing" rather than simply a "writer of stories" that separating thematic purpose from style can be a complex task. To a very high degree, the manner in which the stories are told is closely allied with their matter. And the central position of the storyteller, Philip Marlowe, makes the problem especially difficult.

We should recall first that Chandler's original preference for the detective story resulted largely from the "fundamental dishonesty in the matter of character and motivation" which he perceived in much of contemporary short fiction. Character and motivation are Chandler's, and Marlowe's, abiding interests. Ironically, and irony is a Chandler forté, Marlowe's examination of characters' motives leads him, particularly in the early novels, in a curious circle; their motivations are frequently not unlike his own. But something about the peculiar circumstances in which these individuals find themselves, something in the very nature of the modern world, perverts their actions despite the relative purity of their intentions.

Consider *The Big Sleep*, for example. Vivian Sternwood's initial actions in that novel were clearly honorable according to her own lights; whether she was really trying to protect her sister, her father, herself, or simply the status quo, her intention was clearly "to do the right thing." But because of who she is and the people she must depend on, her efforts lead inevitably to involvement in the parasitic schemes of organized crime. Organized crime shadows the wealthy in Chandler's world, and that symbiotic relationship functions as a leitmotif in many of the novels.

In *Farewell, My Lovely*, a similar situation arises. Moose Malloy is driven by a pure, if simplistic, sense of love—a love that seeks to recapture a vanished past. But his actions, also, become hopelessly entangled with the local rackets operation, although the racketeers here, as in *The Big Sleep*, have little more effect on events than do the novel's other characters. All suffer the common human foibles and are similarly disorganized. Thus, evil, as these stories portray it, is not the consequence of monolithic forces; it is, rather, the composite result of the trifling, unprincipled actions of a variety of corrupt, decadent, or simply unthinking individuals.

In *The High Window*, organized crime has a comparatively minimal role in the book's plot; the personal origins of evil dominate. Mrs. Murdock's imperial presence on her overgrown sunporch is the effete center and moving force of that novel, and her selfishness generates her son's greedy rebellion which culminates in the counterfeiting plot. Her total disregard for others allows the impressionable young Merle Davis slavishly to expiate a crime of which she was not guilty.

*The Lady in the Lake*, with its concern for the "middlemen" (and women) of the system, and its emphasis on coincidence, focuses on the struggle of a woman to escape the tangled web of her own relationships. But it is a self-centered struggle, doomed to prove fruitless—and bloody. *The Little Sister*, on the other hand, manages a delicate balance of motivation between the personal greed of the Quest family and the impersonal, corporate greed of the film world. Again, racketeers figure in the story, but again their actions are fragmented and peripheral to the final resolution.

*The Long Goodbye* offers Chandler's most complex study of individual motives. Marlowe can finally only conjecture about Terry Lennox: "I think maybe the war did it and again I think maybe you were born that way." And so the novel ends, stuck between heredity and environment as explanations for Terry's character. Marlowe may, from his own codified heights, proclaim him a "moral defeatist," but Terry's comment that his behavior is "just an act. . . . An act is all there is" necessitates a more complicated appraisal, to which we must return later.

*Playback*, with its repetition of events and circumstances, is a final display of equivocal motivation: Betty Mayfield, on the run from a crime she did not commit, becomes involved, reluctantly then willingly, in a loose mob power struggle, and Marlowe is left with the depressing feeling that "nothing was any cure but the hard inner heart that asked for nothing from anyone."

Even this cursory recapitulation of the stories reveals Chandler's major thematic interests. In the matter of motive, characters fall roughly into two basic types—those who, though perhaps deluded, act on *what they perceive* to be honorable intentions and those who act out of selfishness, greed, hatred, and expediency. In the earlier novels, the types are more clearly delineated. As the novels progress, ambiguities develop, as do tensions between the way characters expect the world to be and the way it is.

The tension between expectation and fact serves as a central organizing principle in Chandler's stories, and, to reiterate an earlier point, helps explain his use of melodrama and romance, forms with clearly defined, readily frustrated expectations. Chandler, always one to offer a cryptic remark when questioned about the meaning of his stories, once said: "If you have to have significance (the demand for which is the inevitable mark of a half-baked culture), it is just possible that the tensions in a novel of murder are the simplest and yet most complete pattern of the tensions in which we live in this generation." The generation of which he speaks, of course, survived Prohibition, The Great Depression, two world wars, and witnessed both the promise of the California boom and the reality of its urban sprawl and moral decadence. It was a generation thoroughly schooled in the reversal of grand expectations.

It may also be surmised from Chandler's statement that he perceived the detective/mystery novel as an adequate means of exploring the contemporary social ills which are a product of "the tensions in which we live." We may so conclude despite the fact that Chandler once decried interpreting his narrator as a social critic by remarking, "P. Marlowe has as much social conscience as a horse. He has a personal conscience, which is an entirely different matter." But while Marlowe may not be a social critic *per se* (and we must finally deal with the novels' effects on his "personal conscience"), the stories he narrates certainly draw the reader to social conclusions. As Ross Macdonald has put it, the "constant theme" of Chandler's novels "is big-city loneliness, and the wry pain of a sensitive man coping with the roughest elements of a corrupt society." Whether or not Marlowe himself possesses a "social conscience"—and his extremely private existence suggests that, in a sense, he does not—his tales offer substantial material for social interpretation by providing us data on that "corrupt society" which is the source of his loneliness and "wry pain."

Marlowe's turf is a mixed bag of corrupt cops, smug aristocrats, penny-ante grifters, rackets bosses, conceited parents, rebellious children, naive lovers, and related narcissists—all set amidst the blasé decadence of Hollywood and California. In this topsy-turvy world, there is honor among thieves and deceit and greed within families. That love, understanding, and simple humanity are rare commodities in such a world is hardly startling. It is hardly startling, in fact, that love has become so romanticized that characters like Helen Vermilyea, Terry Lennox, and Eileen Wade all suffer from the simplistic notion that "true love never comes but once"—a notion which contributes to their inevitable floundering after past hopes, lost dreams. And it is, in fact, the nauseating inevitability of it all that, typically, leaves Marlowe searching for distraction at a book's end.

That sense of "inevitability" is reinforced by Chandler's heavy-handed, self-conscious reliance on coincidence and fate to develop plots. In *The Big Sleep,* the climactic scene begins: "Fate stage-managed the whole thing." And only a little earlier, as a result of a series of coincidences, Marlowe had stood by helplessly while Harry Jones has met his death at the hands of Canino. That scene, in which Marlowe can only observe the shadows and listen to the voices from the other side of a glass partition, is emblematic of Marlowe's own fated impotence to effect real change in the world. It echoes, in fact, the scene from the first chapter of that book in which he derides the stained-glass knight for his ineffectuality; here Marlowe is likewise "trapped in glass."

The significance of this coincidence-fate-helplessness theme is at least twofold. First, Chandler is genuinely concerned with demonstrating the extent to which Marlowe is influenced by forces beyond his control and, thereby, with defining the limits of his protagonist's romanticism. But secondly, and perhaps more importantly, this overt dependence on fate and coincidence is a basis element of Chandler's parody. He once remarked on the genre's inordinate tendency "when in doubt [to] bring a man through a door with a gun." It is that very sort of mechanical plotting, relying heavily on coincidence, which he parodies by calling attention to it, by using it to excess, and by making it function thematically as a mark of human impotence.

Another thematic device which consistently structures the novels is a conflict between two women. In *The Big Sleep,* we have already noted in detail the relationship between Vivian and Carmen Sternwood. In *Farewell, My Lovely,* the device is less prominent, but the tension between Jessie Florian and Mrs. Grayle is central to that plot's resolution. Without Mrs. Florian's hold over the younger woman, the string of clues which finally unite Moose and Velma could never be unraveled. In *The High Window,* the strange alliance between Mrs. Murdock and Merle Davis is one of that book's primary fascinations. In *The Lady in the Lake,* the formula is equally obvious in the roles of Crystal Kingsley and Mildred Haviland. *The Little Sister* uses sisters again, Mavis Weld and Orfamay Quest, to generate its basic conflict, and a third woman, Delores Gonzales, to further complicate the issue. *The Long Goodbye,* as has also been noted, is set in motion by Eileen Wade's hatred for Sylvia Lennox. *Playback,* in fact, is the only novel which is not organized around some conflict between two women.

Chandler's concentration on the affairs and enmities of women has not gone unnoticed. Michael Mason has argued that Chandler's preference for women as villains "may be explicable simply on the grounds of mystery," and that may well be at least partly true. Doubtless the idea of the murderer proving to be a woman seemed a great deal more novel at the time Chandler began writing than it seems today. But such an explanation for the fact that women are almost invariably the villains provides little or no insight into his use of feminine conflict as a basic structural element. One possible source of illumination on the subject—though it necessarily leads to conjecture and even the "biographical fallacy"—is the author's life.

The first fact to recall is that Chandler grew up in a household of women—his mother, aunt, and grandmother. We know that strife existed in the house, that Chandler termed his grandmother "stupid and arrogant," and it seems safe to project that the household surely had its normal share of disagreements and petty prejudices. It seems likely, in fact, that the household may have had more than its "normal share" of such problems given the "poor relations" status in which we know Chandler and his mother to have been held.

The point is simply that, given his background and experience, Chandler would likely have been more impressed by the rivalries of women than those of men, and that household was surely a powerful shaper of his own psyche. After he grew old enough to leave, he seems still to have had his share of problems with the opposite sex. Despite his rearing in a female household (or perhaps because of it) and despite his thirty relatively content years with Cissy, Chandler was strongly affected by and often mistaken about women at various periods throughout his life. Those of a Freudian bent might say he never resolved the essential question: What does woman want? From his school days in Paris, where (he later recognized) he was totally oblivious to the advances of some of the Parisian schoolgirls, through his various affairs before and during his marriage, to the amazing entanglements in which he found himself after Cissy's death, Chandler always had difficulties dealing with women. His alter ego, Marlowe, has similar, even more pronounced, problems which stem from his dual response to them.

That dual impulse may help explain some of his difficulties and, by extension, those of his creator. Part of the impulse was to protect women, honor them, put them on a pedestal in the manner of the chivalric knight; the other impulse was to separate himself from them lest he be somehow contaminated by a foreignness which he has only vague reasons for fearing. Marlowe demonstrates this ambivalence most dramatically on the second night he finds himself at the home of Anne Riordan in *Farewell, My Lovely*. When she brings him a drink, their fingers touch, and he tells us, in one of his most sentimental remarks, "I held them for a moment and then let go slowly as you let go of a dream when you wake with the sun in your face and have been in an enchanted valley." But only a little later, he rejects her invitation to stay overnight, and insists on going home where he is pleased to find "A homely smell . . . a world where men live, and keep on living." This ambivalence toward women, however, is only one aspect of the essential dualism that marks Marlowe's chief resemblance to his creator. Other features of that dualism have been explored in the previous chapter, but we have yet to examine its centrality in Chandler's work. Marlowe's fascination with chess can help us do that.

At the end of *The High Window*, Marlowe is seeking diversion from an emotionally exhausting case in "beautiful cold remorseless chess, almost creepy in its silent implacability." He is replaying one of the games of the master Capablanca. In this very ordered, predictable setting, he appears to regain his composure. But the effect is short-lived. After playing through the game, he finds himself staring into a mirror and mutters the self-mocking line "You and Capablanca" that closes the book. The scene testifies to Marlowe's own awareness of both the futility of such efforts to order chaotic events and his own drive to make the effort despite its futility.

By *The Long Goodbye*, Marlowe's contempt for his hobby has progressed to the point that he can speak of another master's tournament game which he plays out "seventy-two moves to a draw" as "a prize specimen of the irresistible force meeting the immovable object, . . . and as elaborate a waste of human intelligence as you could find anywhere outside an advertising agency." But despite such disdain, the drive to play the game, for whatever consolation it may offer, is still there.

It is the same need for order, in fact, that determines Marlowe's persistence in his career. Faced with the chaos of human actions, he insists on tracking down its meaning, even though he is constantly confronted with failure and unsatisfying resolutions. Chess is a more orderly analogue of the detective's game, and Marlowe's eventual contempt for it reflects his despair over his own role in the world. It has been said that:

> Man has two primal needs. First is a need for order, peace, and security, for protection against the terror or confusion of life, for a familiar and predictable world, and for a life which is happily more of the same. . . . But the second primal impulse is contrary

> to the first: man positively needs anxiety and uncertainty, thrives
> on confusion and risk, wants trouble, tension, jeopardy, novelty,
> mystery, would be lost without enemies, is sometimes happiest
> when most miserable. Human spontaneity is eaten away by
> sameness: man is the animal most expert at being bored.

Both Chandler and Marlowe recognize this essential dualism, and
each deals with it in his own unique manner.

Chess functions for Marlowe much as the writing process functions for Chandler. Both are artifices of control; both offer at least
the illusion of a momentary order—"remorseless" and "implacable"
—isolated from the ubiquitous chaos. Chandler's very inclusion of
Marlowe's interest in chess and Marlowe's own self-mocking awareness about his hobby both argue, of course, that Chandler was
quite mindful of the ironies of his own creative aims. Both Chandler
and Marlowe recognize finally that their endeavors are doomed to
failure. Order, release from chaos, can not be imposed; to the
extent that it exists, it can only be discovered. Marlowe seems to
think that he has found such order and release in love as *Playback*
ends, but Chandler's intention in *The Poodle Springs Story* was to
debunk that idea as well.

Finally, Chandler's essential theme is writing itself and the
promise of control which that art holds out to the writer. And,
from beginning to end, his work parodies both that promise and the
very genre in which he excelled. Many of the individual examples
of Chandler's self-mockery have already been examined: the knight
in stained glass who establishes a mocking frame in *The Big Sleep;*
Marlowe's "I've never liked this scene" speech in *The Lady in the
Lake;* the use of the Quest family to mock the very idea of romantic
questing in *The Little Sister;* Chandler's self-conscious reliance on
fate and coincidence as plot resolvers, and so on.

But as we pursue the "significant" themes of Chandler's work,
we should bear in mind his caution that such pursuits are "the
inevitable mark of a half-baked culture." That is, such demands for
significance bespeak a desire for simple, clear-cut, easily distilled
"pearls of wisdom." Such demands are, of course, simplistic and,
despite the remarkably simplistic form in which Chandler worked,
part of his message is that significance is not so easily extracted.
Demands for "significance" also suggest a belief that meaning lies

in the language on the page rather than in the relationships between people and the social structures which that language seeks to articulate.

Chandler's response to praise from W. H. Auden may further enlighten the matter. In a 1948 *Harper's* article called "The Guilty Vicarage," Auden had commented:

> Chandler is interested in writing, not detective stories, but serious studies of a criminal milieu, the Great Wrong Place, and his powerful but extremely depressing books should be read and judged not as escape literature, but as works of art.

It is high praise indeed, but Chandler, in a letter to a friend, responded:

> Here I am halfway through a Marlowe story and having a little fun (until I got stuck) and along comes this fellow Auden and tells me I am interested in writing serious studies of a criminal milieu. So now I look at everything I put down and say to myself, Remember, old boy, this has to be a serious study of a criminal milieu. Are you serious? No. Is this a criminal milieu? No, just average corrupt living with the melodramatic angle over-emphasized, not because I am crazy about melodrama for its own sake, but because I am realistic enough to know the rules of the game.

And in the same letter, he asks, "How could I possibly care a button about the detective story as a form? All I'm looking for is an excuse for certain experiments in dramatic dialogue." That is, significance for Chandler lies in characters and in the relationships between them manifested by the language by which they express themselves.

That language reflects his characters' own sense of themselves and of the world. It strives to be at once contemporary and timeless: contemporary in its diction, timeless in its assignation of evil. Henry James, one of Chandler's acknowledged mentors, once wrote that if you can "make the reader *think* the evil for himself . . . you are released from weak specifications," and Chandler follows his lead. He makes his readers "think the evil" by demonstrating, through dialogue, the utterly self-serving depravity that motivates his more malicious characters and which ultimately draws the less malicious into the same human bog. If he is forced by the detective form to detail the "weak specifications" of evil—the murders and pervasive corruption—he does so with an eye to burlesque.

The parody, then, is of the form itself, of all the machinations on which it insists in order to bring its plots to efficient resolution, and of the very human weaknesses on which such demands rest. Chandler fully recognized that such plot demands are not credible, but, as he said, he was "realistic enough to know the rules of the game." The "rules of the game" of writing detective novels required pat, easily grasped endings, and, though he delighted in confusing the issue, he provided them. But his real interests were not so simple; his real interests lay in articulating the complexity of emotions and motives at the base of the modern world. The greed, hate, and delusion which his stories consistently uncover as motives are not, of course, new. They are as old as the human race. What is new in Chandler is the language in which these motives are expressed, and Chandler's experiments with that language created a prose style which is the singular mark of his achievement. Ironically, the genre which allowed him that experimentation and success also trapped him and was partly responsible for his wrenching pessimism.

Chandler began writing detective mysteries for rather simple reasons; he was broke, and the pulp magazines offered him an avenue back into the writing trade as well as the prospect of income. But once he became successful with the genre, he found it impossible to escape it. Because he enjoyed the language experimentation allowed by the fixed form and because he was making money, he kept at it and, for a while, enjoyed himself. But there is ample evidence that, ultimately, the genre itself was a source of frustration and pessimism; that pessimism is reflected both in his stories and in his public remarks and letters. For example, in response to a poor review of *The Little Sister* which ran in the *Atlantic*, he commented: "the better you write a mystery, the more clearly you demonstrate that the mystery is not really worth writing." And, near the end of his life, he wrote: "I am beginning to feel that I have done about all I can do with the mystery story. A writer gets awfully tired of his tricks, or I hope he does—certainly I do. . . ." Within the stories, of course, there is no clearer indication of this sentiment than Marlowe's remark in *The Long Goodbye:* "There is no trap deadlier than the one you set for yourself."

In a sense, Chandler was trapped and knew it. The trap was partly a function of the genre itself and its stylized demands. But the trap was also partly of Chandler's own creation, and Philip Marlowe contributed to it. Marlowe, in fact, is almost as rigid a creation as the form itself. In his knight-errantry and related sensibilities, he is a character whose values are of another age, dropped down amid the relative valuelessness of the present. His ideals are as unyielding as the format of the detective genre. And because Marlowe and his sensibilities are a primary vehicle of meaning for Chandler, Marlowe's very limitations restrict the scope of the novels. The fact that he is a chess player is emblematic of his futile struggle to maintain contact with the possibility of an ordered world.

But if Marlowe's longing is for order, disorder verging on chaos is too often the fact of his existence. And while chess playing testifies to the former, his laughter is often an index of the latter. After killing Canino in *The Big Sleep,* for example, Marlowe tells us he "laughed like a loon." His rare laughter is frequently the result of some such brush with death. His loony, hysterical responses suggest a momentary vision of terror and absurdity. For a brief instant, the fantasies of order, the "fictions in life" which humans create to veil the real world of fact and hatred and death, are ripped aside. Marlowe, in that lunatic moment, comprehends the absurd irrationality beneath the surface of a harsh reality.

But that double vision is not reserved for Marlowe. Terry Lennox is one who—with good reason—lives such a "fiction in life" and says as much, "almost desperately," in his last encounter with Marlowe: "An act is all there is. There isn't anything else." Some of Chandler's own actions, especially late in life, demonstrate a similar awareness. Particularly, his fantastic ride with Natasha Spender in all the pomp of a carnation- and champagne-laden Rolls Royce and formal clothes, and his comment on that occasion—"I appreciate what all of you are doing for me, but I really *want* to die"—give some indication of the theatrical proportions his later life assumed, presumably as a defense against the worries of his reality. Among those worries which he may well have sought to avoid were his own physical maladies, his utter loneliness, and his sense that he had perhaps wasted his talents on an unimportant genre. This kind of "fiction in life" served Chandler to cover his personal nightmares much as laughter often serves Marlowe to mask the unspeakable terror of death. Such a split between fact and act, between coping "normally" with the real world and "making up" an alternative, private reality is one mark of an idealistic mind frustrated by the repulsive truths of the real world. In Chandler's own case, his "act," exemplified by his grotesquely gallant calling for Natasha Spender with carnations and champagne, may be seen as an attempt to re-create in life the noble ideals which he strove to embody in his fiction. By comparison, Terry Lennox's "act" is that of a man striving desperately to gloss over the horrors to which he has already come too close. Both acts partake of the impulse to give order and meaning to life in the face of death.

Typically, crisis situations rip the veil between artifice and actuality, leaving a stark vision of life's absurd end. The crisis of Cissy's death set Chandler off on an extended period of bizarre acts—suicide attempts, rescuing damsels in distress—which finally found some resolution in his acceptance of the certainty of his own death in the company of his good friend Natasha Spender. Terry Lennox's final encounter with Marlowe is the crisis that reveals to him the emptiness of his own life. And Marlowe has his own shocks of recognition of the hairline between reality and absurdity, typically at the muzzle of a gun: laughing "like a loon" after he kills Canino, laughing "like an idiot" at Brody's apartment where guns pop up every time the door opens.

For all these men—Lennox, Marlowe, and Chandler—life itself has become an act, a contrivance, by which to avoid the terror of the death to which they have all stood too close. They deal with the world by making up an alternative reality.

If such "acts," such "made-up" worlds are their only way of coping with the real world, we must consider the implications of this notion for Chandler's novels, which are also, obviously, "made-up" worlds.

For the novelist, of course, the writing process itself is a method for controlling the chaos of reality, for constructing alternative worlds. In his art, even if not always in life, Chandler was in complete control; he was perpetually conscious of the fine line his books walked between realism and absurdity. And we can see that awareness most clearly in the structure of his last great novel, *The Long*

*Goodbye.* In that work, Marlowe is forced finally to confront a dilemma that has plagued other characters in earlier books. He sees the consequences of his own purely motivated gesture come back to haunt him in the form of Señor Maioranos/Terry Lennox.

Marlowe became involved with Lennox initially by simply offering his aid to a man (in this case apparently a "gentleman") in trouble. But that very offer, that simple gesture sprung from the best intentions, is responsible for drawing him into the great morass of the world's troubles, only to find Lennox in the end "a hollow man." Lennox simply can not measure up to Marlowe's code. He is emptied of all but stylized act. He is modern man, scarred by the trauma of world war and unable to live up even to his own ideals. Marlowe's good intentions have only spawned perversion—all the hatred and murder which the book chronicles, actions which might not have happened had he not been trying to uncover the truth for the sake of a friend. The friend proves to be a weak man he cannot respect; the truth is that Marlowe has little or no salving effect on the story's events. In the context of the detective genre, his tale is a parody of our expectations. We expect resolutions to *resolve;* this one only opens up more questions. Marlowe must finally question even his own expectations. He catches himself listening for Lennox's receding footsteps after their sound has died away. "What for?" he asks. "Did I want him to stop suddenly and turn and come back and talk me out of the way I felt?" He feels, we may surmise, betrayed and caught in a situation so complex that he doesn't know what he wants. It is the sort of ambiguity that characterizes Chandler's better work.

Marlowe's ambiguity is, of course, a reflection of Chandler's own, an ambiguity most apparent in some of his parodic remarks about writing. The Hemingway allusions throughout *Farewell, My Lovely,* for example, mock both the profession and the practice of writing; Roger Wade, in *The Long Goodbye,* is a writer who consistently mocks his own craft and writers in general; and the motif pervades the books. In one brief chapter in *The Little Sister,* for example, there are three instances of very self-conscious comments on the subject of writing. One comes when Marlowe is trying to describe Miss Gonzales, the Latin bombshell of the novel. He says: "The smile became soft, lazy and, if you can't think of a better word, provocative." The sentence draws the reader away from the

action to a consideration of the writer's problem of finding the
right word and, indeed, of his frequent inability to bridge the gap
between language and existence.

A similar instance occurs in a conversation between Marlowe
and Mavis Weld in the same chapter. She has recognized him as a
"gum-shoe" and says, "It must have been the smell." To this insult,
Marlowe responds: "I'm beginning to think you write your own
dialogue. . . . I've been wondering just what was the matter with
it." This typical Marlovian wit again focuses our attention on the
writer's difficulty in finding the right words and echoes an authorial
voice complaining that his characters will not behave, that they
have taken to writing their own speeches. And the implication is
that even the author's fictional world is out of control, seeking to
imitate the chaotic real world despite his attempts to restrain it.

The final comment in this chapter on writing comes when Marlowe confronts Mavis Weld. This bit of dialogue ensues; Mavis
speaks first:

> "Out. I don't know you. I don't want to know you. And if I
> did, this wouldn't be either the day or the hour."
> "Never the time and place and the loved one all together," I
> said.
> "What's that?" She tried to throw me out with the point of her
> chin, but even she wasn't that good.
> "Browning. The poet, not the automatic. I feel sure you'd
> prefer the automatic."

The exchange has its sparkle of humor, to be sure, but, in its suggestion that the world has sunk to the point that a major English
poet is only remembered because his name happens to coincide with
that of a gun, the comment does not augur well for the immortality
of poets, and certainly not for pulp detective writers.

In thus burlesqueing his own profession, Chandler acknowledges the likely futility of writing even as he does it. Such self-
mockery calls the writer's own intentions, motivations, and expectations into question. Since Plato, at least, we have assumed that the
writer is motivated largely by a drive for immortality in words.
Chandler's vision, at its bleakest, suggests that such an achievement
is only the last in a long line of delusions which help perpetuate the

sham of order, which help mask the anxiety and terror that would overtake us if we squarely faced the reality of the evil forces loose in the world.

Such sentiments are, of course, not unique to Chandler. T. S. Eliot (whom Chandler also had occasion to mock in *The Long Goodbye*), for one, was another twentieth-century writer capable of such pessimism. Chandler's work bears clear affinities, in fact, with Eliot's "The Hollow Men" (already alluded to in connection with Terry Lennox.) For Chandler, as for Eliot, something not clearly articulable has happened. A shadow has fallen between *motion* and *act*, between *emotion* and *response* (to use Eliot's terms). The continuity linking human emotion, intellect, and moral purpose has been somehow rent asunder. And Chandler's world, like Eliot's, ends not with the bang of organized, orchestrated destruction, but with the whimper of private helplessness in the face of the impending chaos. It is a perverse world, and Chandler's is a black vision. And yet, the writer writes. The human spirit declines to accept its own end.

Perhaps, finally, there is no better explanation of this complex man than the one he penned himself to describe his fictional author, Roger Wade, in *The Long Goodbye:* "He worried about his work and he hated himself because he was just a mercenary hack. He was a weak man, unreconciled, frustrated, but understandable." Obviously, the complexity of the man himself, the internal strife he suffered and the external conflict he witnessed, were responsible for forging the works we now admire, and which surely merit far more attention than those of any mere "mercenary hack."

# Bibliography

*I. Works by Chandler*

A. NOVELS (WITH FIRST AMERICAN PUBLICATION INDICATED)

*The Big Sleep.* New York: Alfred A. Knopf, 1939.
*Farewell, My Lovely.* New York: Alfred A. Knopf, 1940.
*The High Window.* New York: Alfred A. Knopf, 1942.
*The Lady in the Lake.* New York: Alfred A. Knopf, 1943.
*The Little Sister.* Boston: Houghton Mifflin, 1949.
*The Long Goodbye.* Boston: Houghton Mifflin, 1954.
*Playback.* Boston: Houghton Mifflin, 1958.

B. STORIES (WITH FIRST APPEARANCES INDICATED)

"Blackmailers Don't Shoot." *Black Mask*, December 1933.
"Smart-Aleck Kill." *Black Mask*, July 1934.
"Finger Man." *Black Mask*, October 1934.
"Killer in the Rain." *Black Mask*, January 1935.
"Nevada Gas." *Black Mask*, June 1935.
"Spanish Blood." *Black Mask*, November 1935.
"Guns at Cyrano's." *Black Mask*, January 1936.
"The Man Who Liked Dogs." *Black Mask*, March 1936.
"Noon Street Nemesis" (reprinted as "Pick-up on Noon Street"). *Detective Fiction Weekly*, May 30, 1936.
"Goldfish." *Black Mask*, June 1936.
"The Curtain." *Black Mask*, September 1936.

"Try the Girl." *Black Mask*, January 1937.
"Mandarin's Jade." *Dime Detective Magazine*, November 1937.
"Red Wind." *Dime Detective Magazine*, January 1938.
"The King in Yellow." *Dime Detective Magazine*, March 1938.
"Bay City Blues." *Dime Detective Magazine*, June 1938.
"The Lady in the Lake." *Dime Detective Magazine*, January 1939.
"Pearls Are a Nuisance." *Dime Detective Magazine*, April 1939.
"Trouble Is My Business." *Dime Detective Magazine*, August 1939.
"I'll Be Waiting." *Saturday Evening Post*, October 14, 1939.
"The Bronze Door." *Unknown*, November 1939.
"No Crime in the Mountains." *Detective Story*, September 1941.
"Professor Bingo's Snuff." *Park East*, June–August 1951.
"Marlowe Takes on the Syndicate" (reprinted as "The Pencil"). *London Daily Mail*, April 6–10, 1959.

### C. ARTICLES, LETTERS, AND OTHER WORKS

*The Blue Dahlia.* New York: Popular Library, 1976. Reprint of Chandler's 1945 screenplay.
*Chandler Before Marlowe: Raymond Chandler's Early Prose and Poetry, 1908–1912,* ed. Matthew Bruccoli. Columbia: Univ. of South Carolina Press, 1973.
—Reprints Chandler's early verse, essays and reviews.
"Critical Notes," *The Screen Writer*, July 1947.
*The Notebooks of Raymond Chandler and English Summer: A Gothic Romance,* ed. Frank MacShane. New York: The Ecco Press, 1976.
"Oscar Night in Hollywood." *The Atlantic Monthly*, March 1948.
*Raymond Chandler Speaking,* ed. Dorothy Gardiner and Katherine Sorley Walker. 1962; rpt. Boston: Houghton Mifflin, 1977.
—Excerpts from Chandler's letters. Includes the story "A Couple of Writers" and the surviving fragment of *The Poodle Springs Story.*
"The Simple Art of Murder." *The Atlantic Monthly*, December 1944.
—Reprinted in a revised version in *Saturday Review of Literature*, April 15, 1950.
"Ten Per Cent of Your Life." *The Atlantic Monthly*, February 1952.
"Writers in Hollywood." *The Atlantic Monthly*, December 1944.

## II. Selected Works about Chandler

Abrahams, Etta Claire. "Visions and Values in the Action Detective Novel: A Study of the Work of Raymond Chandler, Kenneth Millar, and John D. MacDonald." Unpublished doctoral dissertation, Michigan State University, 1973.

Beekman, E. M. "Raymond Chandler and an American Genre." *Massachusetts Review*, Winter 1973, pp. 149–73.

Boucher, Anthony. "Chandler, Revalued." *New York Times Book Review*, September 4, 1949.

Bruccoli, Matthew, comp. *Raymond Chandler: A Checklist.* Kent, Ohio: Kent State Univ. Press, 1968.

—Extensive bibliographical information, particularly on various editions and printings.

Crider, Allen Billy. "The Private-Eye Hero: A Study of the Novels of Dashiell Hammett, Raymond Chandler, and Ross Macdonald." Unpublished doctoral dissertation, The University of Texas at Austin, 1972.

Durham, Philip. *Down These Mean Streets A Man Must Go.* Chapel Hill: Univ. of North Carolina Press, 1963.

—First book-length study of Chandler.

Elliott, George P. "Country Full of Blondes." *The Nation*, April 23, 1960, pp. 354–60.

Gross, Miriam, ed. *The World of Raymond Chandler.* New York: A & W Publishers, 1978.

—Introduction by Patricia Highsmith. An important collection of essays by friends, acquaintances, and critics—including Julian Symons, Russell Davies, Billy Wilder, Dilys Powell, Michael Mason, Natasha Spender, Jacques Barzun and others.

Houseman, John. "Lost Fortnight." *Harper's Magazine*, August 1965.

Jameson, Fredric. "On Raymond Chandler." *The Southern Review*, Volume 6, 1970, pp. 624–50.

MacShane, Frank. *The Life of Raymond Chandler.* 1976; rpt. New York: Penguin, 1978.

—The definitive biography. First published by E. P. Dutton.

Pendo, Stephen. *Raymond Chandler On Screen: His Novels into Film.* Metuchen, N.J.: Scarecrow Press, 1976.

—Extensive comparisons of novels, screenplays, and finished films.

Pollock, Wilson. "Man With a Toy Gun." *The New Republic*, May 7, 1962, pp. 21–22.

Porter, J. C. "End of the Trail: The American West of Dashiell Hammett and Raymond Chandler." *Western Historical Quarterly*, October 1975, pp. 411–24.

Reck, T. S. "Raymond Chandler's Los Angeles." *The Nation*, December 20, 1975, pp. 661–63.

Ruhm, Herbert. "Raymond Chandler: From Bloomsbury to the Jungle—and Beyond." In David Madden, ed., *Tough Guy Writers of the Thirties.* Carbondale: Southern Illinois Univ. Press, 1968.

Russell, D. C. "The Chandler Books." *The Atlantic,* March 1945.

Sington, Derrick. "Raymond Chandler on Crime and Punishment." *The Twentieth Century,* May 1959, pp. 502–4.


## III. Selected Works of General Relevance

Auden, W. H. "The Guilty Vicarage." *Harper's Magazine,* May 1948.

Ball, John, ed. *The Mystery Story.* San Diego: University Extension, University of California, 1976.
—A collection of essays. Includes one by James Sandoe, a Chandler correspondent, which provides information on early paperback collections of Chandler's stories.

Barzun, Jacques and Wendell Hertig Taylor. *A Catalogue of Crime.* New York: Harper and Row, 1971.
—Includes brief critical assessments of Chandler's novels. Prefers *The Lady in the Lake.*

Brophy, Brigid. "Detective Fiction: A Modern Myth of Violence?" *The Hudson Review,* Spring 1965, pp. 11–30.

Byrd, Max. "The Detective Detected: From Sophocles to Ross Macdonald." *Yale Review,* October 1974, pp. 72–83.

Cawelti, John G. *Adventure, Mystery, and Romance: Formula Stories as Art and Popular Culture.* Chicago: Univ. of Chicago Press, 1976.
—Examines the artistic and cultural importance of "formula stories." Devotes a chapter to "Hammett, Chandler, and Spillane." Includes extensive bibliographical notes.

Hartman, Geoffrey H. "Literature High and Low: The Case of the Mystery Story." In *The Fate of Reading and Other Essays.* Chicago: Univ. of Chicago Press, 1975.

Haycraft, Howard, ed. *The Art of the Mystery Story: A Collection of Critical Essays.* New York: Simon and Schuster, 1946.
—A standard collection. Reprints "The Simple Art of Murder."

Hugo, Grant. "The Political Influence of the Thriller." *Contemporary Review,* December 1972, pp. 284–89.

Hutter, Albert D. "Dreams, Transformations, and Literature: The Implications of Detective Fiction." *Victorian Studies,* December 1975, pp. 181–209.

Macdonald, Ross. *On Crime Writing.* Santa Barbara: Capra Press, 1973.
—Includes "The Writer as Detective Hero," in which Macdonald discusses Chandler and Marlowe.

Maugham, Somerset. "The Decline and Fall of the Detective Story." In *The Vagrant Mood.* London: Heinemann, 1952.

Murch, A. E. *The Development of the Detective Novel.* London: Peter Owen, 1958.

Poirier, Richard. *A World Elsewhere: The Place of Style in American Literature.* New York: Oxford Univ. Press, 1966.

Porte, Joel. *The Romance in America: Studies in Cooper, Poe, Hawthorne, Melville and James.* Middletown, Conn.: Wesleyan Univ. Press, 1969.

Symons, Julian. *Bloody Murder—From the Detective Story to the Crime Novel: A History.* London: Penguin, 1972.

Todorov, Tzvetan. *The Poetics of Prose.* Ithaca, N.Y.: Cornell Univ. Press, 1977. Richard Howard, trans.
—Devotes a chapter to "The Typology of Detective Fiction."

Truffaut, François, with the collaboration of Helen G. Scott. *Hitchcock.* New York: Simon and Schuster, 1967.

# Notes

References are identified by the page number and last three words of each quotation. Notes to Chandler's works are included only where the reference cannot be readily determined from the text.

## Chapter 1

| PAGE | QUOTE | SOURCE |
|---|---|---|
| 1 | also be contempt | Chandler, letter to Alfred Knopf, January 12, 1946. |
| 2 | an "utter swine" | Chandler, letter to Leroy Wright, March 31, 1957. |
| 2 | and arrogant grandmother | Chandler, letter to Hamish Hamilton, July 15, 1954. |
| 2 | to gain approval | Natasha Spender, "His Own Long Goodbye," in *The World of Raymond Chandler*, edited by Miriam Gross (New York: A&W Publishers, 1978), 128–59. |
| 3 | too full of | Chandler, letter to Hamish Hamilton, November 10, 1950. |
| 3 | and tyrannical uncle | Autobiographical statement from Chandler files. Quoted by Frank MacShane, *The Life of Raymond Chandler* (New York: Penguin, 1978), p. 12, hereafter referred to as *The Life*. |
| 4 | of Mandarin Chinese | MacShane, *The Life*, p. 13. |
| 4 | without a country | Chandler, letter to Hamish Hamilton, December 11, 1950. |

| PAGE | QUOTE | SOURCE |
|---|---|---|
| 4 | any time now | Chandler, letter to Wesley Hart, November 11, 1950. |
| 5 | they ever had | Interview with Rene MacColl, *Daily Express*, April 25, 1955. Quoted by MacShane, in *The Life*, p. 17. |
| 5 | art, and meditation | MacShane, *The Life*, p. 16. |
| 5 | so infinitely better | Chandler, letter to Hamish Hamilton, December 11, 1950. |
| 5 | and vile dust | Chandler, in Matthew Bruccoli, ed., *Chandler Before Marlowe* (Columbia: Univ. of South Carolina Press, 1973), p. 67. |
| 5 | nasty in tone | Chandler, letter to Hamish Hamilton, April 9, 1949. |
| 6 | hours a week | Chandler, letter to Hamish Hamilton, November 10, 1950. |
| 6 | a British uniform | Autobiographical statement from Chandler files. Quoted by MacShane, in *The Life*, p. 27. |
| 7 | world gone leprous | Raymond Chandler collection, UCLA. Quoted by MacShane, in *The Life*, p. 29. |
| 7 | the same again | Chandler, letter to Deirdre Gartrell, July 25, 1957. |
| 7 | didn't get anywhere | Stanley Kunitz, ed., *Twentieth Century Authors, First Supplement* (1955), entry for Chandler. |
| 8 | they knew it | Chandler, letter to Helga Greene, May 5, 1957. |
| 9 | always on guard | MacShane, *The Life*, p. 36. |
| 9 | anything for granted | Chandler to Cyril Ray, interview, *Sunday Times*, September 21, 1952. |
| 9 | character and motivation | Chandler, letter to George Harmon Cox, April 9, 1939. |
| 10 | I was learning | Chandler, letter to Hamish Hamilton, November 10, 1950. |
| 10 | over crime solution | Joseph Shaw, ed., *The Hard-Boiled Omnibus*, 1952, p. viii. Quoted by MacShane, in *The Life*, p. 46. |
| 10 | a poor plotter | From an interview with Irving Wallace in Los Angeles, August 24, 1945. Quoted in *Raymond Chandler Speaking*, Dorothy Gardiner and Katherine |

| PAGE | QUOTE | SOURCE |
|------|-------|--------|
| | | Sorley Walker, eds., (Boston: Houghton Mifflin, 1977), p. 216. |
| 10 | plots appalls me | Chandler, letter to Charles Morton, November 20, 1944. |
| 10 | the last chapter | Chandler, letter to Joseph Sistrom, December 16, 1947. |
| 11 | for the fun | From Chandler's notebooks. Quoted in *Raymond Chandler Speaking*, pp. 207–9. |
| 12 | almost unparalleled stupidity | Chandler, letter to Ray Stark, June 8, 1948. |
| 12 | acid, sour, grouchy | "On the Fourth Floor of the Paramount," interview with Billy Wilder by Ivan Moffatt, in *The World of Raymond Chandler*, p. 48. |
| 12 | life for me | John Houseman, "Lost Fortnight," *Harper's*, August 1965, pp. 55–61. |
| 13 | had no ending | Ibid., p. 58. |
| 13 | an astonishing proposal | Ibid., p. 59. |
| 14 | mouthful of popcorn | Chandler files. Quoted by MacShane, in *The Life*, p. 173. |
| 15 | need me for | Quoted by François Truffaut in *Hitchcock* (New York: Simon and Schuster, 1967), p. 142. |
| 15 | by filling orders | Chandler, letter to Carl Brandt, December 21, 1950. |
| 16 | nightmare of mourning | Spender, "His Own Long Goodbye," p. 128. |
| 16 | with a lady | Ibid. |
| 16 | Don Quixote illusions | Ibid., p. 129. |
| 16 | white silk scarf | Ibid., p. 141. |
| 16 | *want* to die | Ibid. |
| 17 | lonely old eagle | Chandler, letter to Hamish Hamilton, January 5, 1950. |

## Chapter 2

| 20 | confused story line | Stephen Pendo, *Raymond Chandler on Screen: His Novels into Film* (Metuchen, N.J.: Scarecrow, 1976), p. 38. |
| 20 | concatenation of circumstances | Chandler, letter to Alfred Knopf, February 19, 1939. |

| PAGE | QUOTE | SOURCE |
|------|-------|--------|
| 44 | it indefinitely otherwise | Chandler, letter to Blanche Knopf, March 15, 1942. |
| 44 | levels of interest | Russell Davies, "Omnes Me Impune Lacessunt," in *The World of Raymond Chandler*, p. 35. |

## Chapter 3

| | | |
|------|-------|--------|
| 52 | a materialistic world | MacShane, *The Life*, p. 102. |
| 57 | the human race | Anthony Boucher, "Chandler Revalued," *New York Times Book Review*, September 4, 1949. |
| 57 | that comes through | Chandler, letter to James Sandoe, October 14, 1949. |
| 58 | real Hollywood novel | MacShane, *The Life*, p. 150. |
| 60 | a proper mystery | Chandler, letter to James Sandoe, May 3, 1949. |

## Chapter 4

| | | |
|------|-------|--------|
| 65 | not without censure | Spender, "His Own Long Goodbye," p. 135. |
| 66 | or plain foolish | Chandler, letter to Bernice Baumgarten, May 14, 1952. |
| 76 | we live in | Chandler, letter to Bernice Baumgarten, May 14, 1952. |
| 78 | been called undistinguished | Anthony Boucher, quoted by Philip Durham, in *Down These Mean Streets a Man Must Go: Raymond Chandler's Knight* (Chapel Hill: Univ. of North Carolina Press, 1963), p. 133. |
| 78 | a forgettable work | Michael Mason, "Marlowe, Men and Women," in *The World of Raymond Chandler*, p. 100. |
| 78 | hoked-up job | George P. Elliott, "Country Full of Blondes," *The Nation*, April 23, 1960, pp. 354–60. |
| 80 | mound and weep | Chandler, letter to Charles Morton, October 9, 1950. |
| 81 | with amorous interludes | Chandler, letter to Wilbur Smith, October 16, 1958. |

## Chapter 5

| PAGE | QUOTE | SOURCE |
|------|-------|--------|
| 88 | real dramatic development | Chandler, letter to George Kull, February 3, 1948. |
| 95 | of the novelettes | Chandler, letter to James Sandoe, October 9, 1950. |
| 95 | base commercial motive | Ibid. |

## Chapter 6

| PAGE | QUOTE | SOURCE |
|------|-------|--------|
| 106 | worth living in | Chandler, "The Simple Art of Murder," in *The Atlantic Monthly*, December 1944, p. 59. |
| 106 | and bad guys | Ross Macdonald, "The Writer as Detective Hero," in *On Crime Writing* (Santa Barbara, Calif.: Capra Press, 1973), pp. 9–24. |
| 106 | writing is overstated | Chandler, letter to Howard Haycraft, December 9, 1946. |
| 106 | put him there | Chandler, letter to Mr. Inglis, October 1951. |
| 107 | full of whiskey | Ibid. |
| 108 | rent was low | *The Long Goodbye*, Chapter 1. |
| 109 | a literal nonentity | Davies, "Omnes Me Impune Lacessunt," in *The World of Raymond Chandler*, p. 33. |
| 109 | being the hero | Clive James, "The Country Behind the Hill," in *The World of Raymond Chandler*, p. 126. |
| 110 | it "morally obtuse" | Mason, "Marlowe, Men and Women," p. 95. |
| 111 | is a man | Gershon Legman, *Love and Death: A Study in Censorship*. Quoted by Michael Mason, p. 97. |
| 111 | other than homosexual | Quoted by Michael Mason, in "Marlowe, Men and Women," p. 99. |
| 111 | conventional woman hating | Geoffrey H. Hartmann, "Literature High and Low: The Case of the Mystery Story," in *The Fate of Reading and Other Essays* (Chicago: Univ. of Chicago Press, 1975), pp. 203–222. |
| 111 | lenient towards men | Mason, "Marlowe, Men and Women," p. 95. |

| PAGE | QUOTE | SOURCE |
|------|-------|--------|
| 114 | what he will | Davies, "Omnes Me Impune Laces-sunt," in *The World of Raymond Chandler*, p. 33. |
| 115 | no world's goods | Sir Thomas Malory, *Morte Darthur*, Book I, Chapter 6. |
| 115 | a single entity | Max Byrd, "The Detective Detected: From Sophocles to Ross Macdonald," *Yale Review*, 44 (October 1974), pp. 72–83. |
| 116 | what's the matter | *The Long Goodbye*, Chapter 39. |

## Chapter 7

| | | |
|------|-------|--------|
| 117 | who write writing | Quoted by MacShane, in *The Life*, p. 72. |
| 118 | leave an afterglow | Chandler, letter to Alfred Knopf, January 12, 1946. |
| 118 | they can understand | Chandler, letter to H. N. Swanson, September 22, 1954. |
| 118 | man at that | Chandler, "The Simple Act of Murder," p. 58. |
| 118 | somebody's party line | Chandler, letter to Dale Warren, January 7, 1945. |
| 118 | is the bunk | Chandler, letter to James Sandoe, December 16, 1944. |
| 119 | of the description | Chandler, letter to Helga Greene, April 30, 1957. |
| 120 | from his fingers | Chandler, letter to Frederick Lewis Allen, May 7, 1948. |
| 121 | Chandler believed in | MacShane, *The Life*, p. 93. |
| 121 | first person narrative | Davies, "Omne Me Impune Laces-sunt," in *The World of Raymond Chandler*, p. 32. |
| 121 | voice of Marlowe | Macdonald, "The Writer as Detective Hero," p. 19. |
| 122 | they are phoney | Chandler, letter to Dale Warren, January 7, 1945. |
| 124 | gets into print | Chandler, letter to Alex Barris, March 18, 1949. |
| 126 | simple visual image | Chandler, letter to James Sandoe, April 14, 1959. |
| 126 | as a breadstick | *The Big Sleep*, Chapter 26. |

| PAGE | QUOTE | SOURCE |
|------|-------|--------|
| 126 | a wood rasp | *The Lady in the Lake,* Chapter 5. |
| 126 | as a grapefruit | *The Lady in the Lake,* Chapter 4. |
| 126 | in a snowbank | *The Long Goodbye,* Chapter 2. |
| 126 | lonely as lighthouses | *The Little Sister,* Chapter 19. |
| 126 | shadows on grass | *Farewell, My Lovely,* Chapter 2. |
| 126 | in the moonlight | *The Long Goodbye,* Chapter 47. |
| 126 | a parking meter | *Playback.* |
| 126 | side of beef | *The High Window.* |
| 126 | a split lip | *The Little Sister.* |
| 126 | of angel food | *Farewell, My Lovely.* |
| 127 | a down payment | *The Little Sister.* |
| 127 | refusing a loan | *The High Window.* |
| 127 | little tangled grammar | Ibid. |
| 128 | give them one | Richard Poirier, *A World Elsewhere: The Place of Style in American Literature* (New York: Oxford Univ. Press, 1966), p. ix. |
| 128 | the American mind | James, "The Country Behind the Hill," in *The World of Raymond Chandler,* p. 117. |
| 131 | be first-rate | Elliott, "Country Full of Blondes," *The Nation,* April 23, 1960, p. 355. |
| 131 | of the day | Poirier, pp. 11–12. |
| 131 | without destroying it | Quoted by MacShane, in *The Life,* p. 51. |
| 131 | assault the citadel | Introduction to *Trouble is My Business.* |

## Chapter 8

| | | |
|------|-------|--------|
| 133 | character and motivation | Chandler, letter to George Hamilton Cox, April 9, 1939. |
| 135 | in this generation | Chandler, letter to James Sandoe, October 17, 1948. |
| 136 | entirely different matter | Chandler, letter to Dale Warren, January 7, 1946. |
| 136 | a corrupt society | Macdonald, "The Writer as Detective Hero," p. 19. |
| 137 | grounds of mystery | Mason, "Marlowe, Men and Women," p. 91. |

| PAGE | QUOTE | SOURCE |
|------|-------|--------|
| 140 | at being bored | Harry Berger, Jr. "Naive Consciousness and Culture Change: An Essay in Historical Structuralism," *Bulletin of the Midwest Modern Language Association,* 6 (Spring 1973), p. 35. |
| 141 | works of art | W. H. Auden, "The Guilty Vicarage," *Harper's Magazine,* May 1948, p. 408. |
| 141 | of the game | Chandler, letter to Frederick Lewis Allen, May 7, 1948. |
| 141 | in dramatic dialogue | Ibid. |
| 141 | from weak specifications | Quoted by Joel Porte in *The Romance in America* (Middletown: Wesleyan Univ. Press, 1969), p. 212. |
| 142 | really worth writing | Chandler, letter to Hamish Hamilton, October 5, 1949. |
| 142 | certainly I do | Chandler, letter to Edward Weeks, February 27, 1957. |

# Index

163